The Love That Sets You Free

Rachel Lin

© **Copyright 2024 - All rights reserved.**

The content contained within this book may not be reproduced, duplicated, or transmitted without direct written permission from the author or the publisher.

Under no circumstances will any blame or legal responsibility be held against the publisher or author for any damages, reparation, or monetary loss due to the information contained within this book, either directly or indirectly.

Legal Notice:

This book is copyright-protected. It is only for personal use. You cannot amend, distribute, sell, use, quote, or paraphrase any part, or the content within this book without the author's or publisher's consent.

Disclaimer Notice:

Please note the information contained within this document is for educational and entertainment purposes only. All effort has been executed to present accurate, up-to-date, reliable, and complete information. No warranties of any kind are declared or implied. Readers acknowledge that the author is not engaged in rendering legal, financial, medical, or professional advice. The content within this book has been derived from various sources. Please consult a licensed professional before attempting any techniques outlined in this book.

By reading this document, the reader agrees that under no circumstances is the author responsible for any direct or indirect losses incurred as a result of the use of the information contained within this document, including, but not limited to, errors, omissions, or inaccuracies.

Table of Contents

Introduction 3
PART 1 I Wanna Know What Love Is 5
Chapter 1: Love Makes You Do Crazy Things 7
Chapter 2: My Story–What I Learned About Love 15
Chapter 3: What Others Say 29
PART 2 Barriers to Love 41
Chapter 4: Patriarchy's Influence on Love 43
Chapter 5: Romantic Love 51
Chapter 6: Unrequited Love 55
Chapter 7: The "Glass Ceiling" of Love 59
Chapter 8: Selling Out for Love 63
Chapter 9: Codependency 67
Chapter 10: W.R.D. Fairbairn–Theory of Object Relations 71
Chapter 11: Toxic Love 75
PART 3 The Love That Sets You Free 95
Chapter 12: Love Is All There Is 97
Chapter 13: Self-love Is the Foundation 99
Chapter 14: Unconditional Love 109
Chapter 15: Differentiation of Self 117
Chapter 16: Love in a Mature Relationship 119
Chapter 17: Compassion 125
Chapter 18: Forgiveness 129
Chapter 19: Gratitude 133

Chapter 20: Love Expressed in Work	135
PART 4 Love Rules	141
Chapter 21: The ABCs of a Happy, Healthy, Fulfilling Relationship	143
Author Bio	159
References	161

Trigger warning: This book contains topics including discrimination, assault, abuse, and domestic violence. Readers who may be unsettled by these topics should proceed with caution.

Introduction

Love is an enigma, a kaleidoscope of emotions, experiences, and expectations. To distill it into a singular definition accessible to all is a formidable task. Yet, within these pages, I embark on precisely that journey—to craft a compass through the labyrinthine complexities of love, guiding us toward a shared understanding and agreement that we all need, want, and deserve love, sanity, safety, peace, respect, support, and compassion. We all need, want, and deserve to be seen, heard, and gotten. We all deserve to be free from harm, abuse, violence, humiliation, and degradation.

In this endeavor, I offer not merely a manual, but a beacon—a guiding light illuminating the path through a myriad of perceptions, societal norms, and personal histories. Together, we navigate through the entanglement of ideas, attitudes, and projections toward a destination we collectively yearn for—a love that is as indispensable as it is elusive.

At its essence, this book is a manifesto—a call to arms to reclaim a love that not only sustains us but propels us towards our fullest potential. It is a love that serves as a steadfast ally, nurturing our authenticity, fostering our wholeness, and empowering us to embrace our inherent magnificence and all that we are. It is the key to our joy, wholeness, and aliveness. It is the greatest gift we can give to ourselves and to the world. Mastery in the game of love means a win for everyone.

Yet, such liberation does not come without its trials. It is amid the crucible of adversity that we forge our truest selves—confronting our shadows, navigating our vulnerabilities, and emerging strengthened by the very challenges we face.

Join me on this odyssey—an exploration that traverses the landscapes of confusion and the depths of pain—to arrive in the fabled "promised land" of love. Here, amid the trials and tribulations, lies the transformative power of love—the love that sets us free.

Together, let us embark on this exhilarating voyage—one that liberates, uplifts, nurtures, heals, and ultimately empowers us to embrace the boundless possibilities of love's embrace.

PART 1

I Wanna Know What Love Is

Chapter 1:
Love Makes You Do Crazy Things

Love makes you do crazy things. –Will Smith

***

It was called "the slap that was heard around the world." On March 27, 2022, at the 94th Academy Awards, comedian Chris Rock was about to present an award when he told a joke about Jada Pinkett-Smith's baldness (oblivious to the fact that she has alopecia, an autoimmune disorder that causes hair loss): "Jada, I love you. G.I. Jane II--can't wait to see it!" Everyone laughed, except Jada, who was not amused. Her husband, Will Smith, stopped laughing as soon as he saw her roll her eyes. To everyone's surprise, Will got up on the stage and slapped Chris hard across the face. Everyone was stunned, but no one came to remove Will Smith for violating the Academy's code of conduct.

Thereafter, Chris continued with his presenting duties with great composure and professionalism. Later that evening, Will Smith won the Best Actor award for King Richard, a film about the father of the tennis superstars, Venus and Serena Williams. Jada was seen laughing after the attack, a clear sign that she accepts this display of chivalry, this kind of behavior as proof of his love and devotion. The character Will portrayed in King Richard was a fierce defender of his family. Will said he was overwhelmed with what God was calling on him to do and to be in this world. He was called to love and protect people. He said he wanted to be a vessel and ambassador for love.

He apologized to the Academy and to his nominees, but not to Chris, probably because he felt justified in doing what he did. He suggested that art imitates life—like the crazy father he portrayed, saying, "love will make you do crazy things." But the Williams' father never hit anyone in the film. Will blamed just about everything and everybody but himself. God made him do it, overwhelming him with demands. Satan made him do it, just as Denzel Washington warned him:

"At your highest moment, that's when the Devil comes for you." Love made him do it. The desire to protect Jada made him do it. His association with the character in the movie made him do it. For this Oscar-worthy speech (2022), the audience gave him a standing ovation.

>What about you?
>
>What crazy things would love make you do?
>
>What would you do for love?
>
>What wouldn't you do for love?
>
>What would you be ready to sacrifice for love?
>
>Who would you be willing to betray for love?
>
>What is more important to you: to belong or to be authentic?
>
>Who took your shine? Why did you allow it?

Love Suffers from a Case of Mistaken Identity

I think the problem with love lies in general confusion about what it is. We are different people with different needs, and we come up with different definitions, ideas, ideals, experiences, and expectations of love. With love, there is no one-size-fits-all. What love is to one person might be smothering or engulfment or control to another. It comes down to what lessons we learned and what messages and experiences we were exposed to while growing up, which mostly add to the confusion. One thing I'm clear about is we need to release love from the expectation and burden of making us feel better.

It's really hard to agree on much. I think love suffers mostly from a case of mistaken identity when what we need is a universal definition of love that would work for everyone. Otherwise, it will be a constant source of headaches and heartaches, of unfulfillment and unmet expectations. Just like considering money to be the root of all evil would not result in a healthy, functional, responsible relationship with money, if we were to mistake a pen for a microphone or vice-versa, we shouldn't be surprised if neither item does what it's intended to. As I ponder this question, what springs to mind is the Indian parable of "The Blind Men and the Elephant" (Saxe, 1873).

A group of six blind men heard that a strange animal, called an elephant, had been brought to their town, but none of them knew of its shape and form. They said, "Since we are capable of touch, we will inspect it and get to know it this way." So, they approached the elephant and groped about it.

The first man, whose hand landed on the trunk, said, "The elephant is like a thick snake." The second man, whose hand reached its ear, said it was like a giant fan. To the third man, whose hand was upon its leg, the elephant was like a pillar or a tree. To the fourth man, who placed his hand upon its side, the elephant was a wall. The fifth man, who felt its tail, described the elephant as a rope. The last man felt its tusk and claimed the elephant was hard and smooth like a spear. Each man touched a completely different part of the animal, and each concluded he was right. This led to a loud disagreement. Each was only partially right, as this does not accurately and adequately describe the elephant.

We humans often tend to take our partial experiences as a whole truth, and our individual perspectives as the only version of reality. Perhaps if we put all the parts together, we may get closer to the truth. The moral of this parable is that people tend to claim absolute truth based on their limited, subjective experience while rejecting others' equally limited and partial truths. As applied to love, one's idea of love is neither right nor wrong but, rather, is subjective based on one's maturity, values, beliefs, experiences, personal evolution, perspectives, and convictions, as well as past pain, trauma, and unmet needs from childhood.

Love might mean a Birken bag to one, or a Ferrari to another. It might mean being taken care of financially and not having to grow up or face adult responsibilities. For many, love is a transaction where we give to get. Melania Trump was once asked by a New York University business student if she would still be with Donald Trump if he weren't rich. "If I weren't beautiful, do you think he'd be with me?" she quipped. What I am aiming for with this book is a universal definition of love that would set us free—one that empowers, nurtures, liberates, and heals. It is the wind in our sails; it includes, embraces, and celebrates all that we are: our beauty and our warts, our vulnerabilities and our strengths, our truths and our mistakes. This love should embrace our awesomeness, brilliance, imperfections, doubts, and fears, all we want and need to thrive, and all that brings out the best in us. This love allows us to be happily, fully, and authentically who we are, with no judgment and no apology.

We don't just want a part of the elephant; we want the whole damn elephant and more! We all need and deserve to be loved, accepted, respected, nurtured, cherished, and safe. We want all the love and power essential to developing into loving people, who can contribute to a happy, safe, healthy, beautiful, and compassionate world. We want to fill ourselves up completely with this kind of love so that we may, in turn, joyfully and freely extend it to others. Yes, let's dream big. You know this is the love that you need and want and deserve, and you should not settle for anything less!

If we were to regard love as a game, when it's played right, it would be one where everyone wins—you, your partner, your children, your friends, your community, and the world. There would be no agenda, no manipulation, no humiliation, no control, no domination, no prejudice, no violence, no gaslighting, no aggression, no disrespect, and no abuse in any form, be it physical, emotional, psychological, or spiritual.

This love would only show up as our sharing, giving, caring, respecting, protecting, supporting, and honoring one another.

The Hero's Journey

Here's what love might look like, if we were to apply the 12 stages of Joseph Campbell's "The Hero's Journey" framework to the theme of learning about love (Campbell, 1949). It can provide an interesting perspective on the emotional and personal growth involved in the process.

The "Hero's Journey" might be adapted to the context of love as follows:

The Ordinary World

The hero (or in this case, the individual seeking to learn about love) begins in their ordinary world—at home, alone, safe, and missing nothing.

The Call to Adventure

The hero has a sense of wanting something more or having a desire for deeper connection and personal evolution.

Refusal of the Call

At this stage, the individual may be hesitant or resistant to exploring love. They might have fears, doubts, or past experiences that make them reluctant to embark on this journey.

Meeting the Mentor

The hero encounters someone who can guide them on their journey to understanding love. This mentor could be a friend, family member, therapist, or even a book or resource that provides insights into relationships and love.

Crossing the Threshold

The individual decides to take the plunge into the world of love. They enter the dating scene or actively seek opportunities to connect with others romantically.

Tests, Allies, and Enemies

In the realm of love, the individual encounters various challenges and experiences. These could include dating disappointments, heartbreaks, betrayals, but also positive experiences and the support of friends and loved ones.

Approach to the Innermost Cave

The hero delves deeper into their own emotions and vulnerabilities. They may need to confront their own insecurities, past traumas, and fears related to love.

Ordeal

This represents a significant challenge or crisis in the individual's romantic life. It might be a major breakup, a difficult decision about a relationship, or a moment of deep self-reflection.

Reward (Seizing the Sword)

After facing the ordeal and learning from their experiences, the individual gains insights into love and relationships. They may discover what they truly want and need in a partner, in a relationship, and in themselves.

The Road Back

The individual decides what to do with their newfound understanding of love. They may choose to continue searching for love, make changes in their existing relationships, work through childhood traumas and limiting beliefs, and/or decide to focus on self-love and personal growth.

Resurrection

This stage symbolizes a transformation in the individual's perception and approach to love. They may be more open, compassionate, and willing to embrace the complexities of love.

Return With the Elixir

Having learned about love through their journey, the individual returns to their ordinary world with a deeper understanding of themselves and their capacity to love. They may be better equipped to build and maintain healthy relationships.

"The Hero's Journey" is a flexible framework applied here for learning about love in a metaphorical way to explore the emotional and personal growth that can come from romantic experiences, where unwanted parts of us can finally show up to be made whole, complete, and healed. Love is a complex and deeply personal subject, and everyone's journey will be unique.

Chapter 2:

My Story–
What I Learned About Love

I was born in a little village in Guangdong, China, by caesarian section, weighing 8-1/2 pounds, for which my mother never forgave me, insisting I had ruined her body. My thought at the age of six, upon seeing her naked body, was, "Gee, I didn't know one could get cellulite from giving birth that way." She stopped breastfeeding me very early as she insisted I hurt her. My father left for the US shortly after I was born, so I had practically no memory of him. He went ahead with the intention of sending for Mother and then me, once he got settled and cleared whatever red tape he needed to clear. Mother left sometime before I turned two. I lived in a wonderful house with an open courtyard in the center with my paternal grandmother, whose job was to look after me until it was time for me to join my parents in San Francisco.

She quickly fell ill and was no longer available to play with me past the age of one. Our favorite game was her letting me sit on the crossed feet of her fully extended legs and pulling me up and down, almost like a seesaw. By age one, she said I was too heavy for this game, and she stopped playing with me altogether. I don't remember having any playmates. I made my own toys and entertained myself for the most part. I remember developing very quickly—talking, walking, and toilet-trained by age one; village gossip and storyteller by age two.

My grandmother was desperate for me to grow up fast, as she knew she was dying and would not be around much longer. She would beat me for not learning to read and write Chinese fast enough at the age of two. Some of the village women (my friends) witnessed this and cried for me. I don't remember crying much. I resented having to learn when I'd rather be playing or visiting my adult friends.

My childhood in China, or the first 3-1/2 years of my life, was idyllic. Since my parents and grandmother were either gone or unavailable, my village became my mother. My village replaced the nuclear family. For me, "mother" was not limited to a person; it was an environment of love, safety, warmth, appreciation, respect, and welcome. It felt like basking in eternal sunshine. I lived in a beautiful place surrounded by kind and wonderful people who loved and cherished me. I had everything I needed and wanted; I was missing nothing. I never felt abandoned, stranded, or lost, nor did I feel coddled or pitied for having no parents around. I never missed my parents. People were telling me I would soon be reunited with my parents, and I only pretended to feel that this was a good thing. Whenever I got tired of Grandmother and her outrageous expectations and restrictions, which was often, I would put on my straw hat with the wide brim and "go visiting," and I might not return the same day. I always seemed to know exactly where to go whenever I felt hungry, tired, or needed company. I would run errands with my aunt, who was often my companion. I would visit mothers with newborns, get delicious dried fruit from the herbalists, and spend afternoons in the opium dens with the men, entertaining them with bits of nonsense and gossip I made up. I did whatever I wanted when I wanted, stopped only by Grandmother.

It's been said that it takes a village to raise a child. But in my case, it also took this child to raise a village. I felt loved, respected, accepted, safe, and cherished by the villagers. Around them, I was smart, entertaining, special, and significant. I felt certain that I was the favorite child, that I belonged, that I mattered, that my thoughts and feelings mattered, and that I was an important part of the community. I was someone who had a contribution to make and a "job" to do: bringing people together and keeping the village peaceful and happy. All that was expected of me was to focus on being a carefree and happy child, to play, to grow, and to develop. I don't know when exactly the process of differentiation took place, but I remember always feeling distinct from others, being my own person with my own feelings and thoughts. I was opinionated, territorial, and outspoken. The only person to tell me that it was not OK to be me and to talk and act the way I did was Grandmother, whom I usually did not heed. I remember telling my aunt that putting a man to death for stealing was not justice and that grown-ups really shouldn't be lighting firecrackers during Chinese New Year (because it meant I had to arrange to leave my village on those days to get away from the awful noise). I told a strange woman that she was not allowed to take melons from my orchard (not realizing it was communal property). I don't remember getting any special treatment as a child without parents. I had it all. I don't remember ever experiencing any lack or feelings of sadness, jealousy, anger, loss, rejection, or abandonment. I knew of the existence of my parents, but I did not need them or miss them. I had everything I needed right here in this paradise. I enjoyed a childhood that few children have ever experienced, and I think this did wonders for my self-esteem and confidence and helped me survive the onslaught of childhood abuse that was to come. My first few years in China literally saved my life.

While the villagers doted on me and accepted me exactly as I was, Grandmother saw things differently. I was a bit too free and wild for her tastes, and I would not grow up fast enough for her. It was as if she expected me to grow up and be self-sufficient as quickly as possible because she was dying. She didn't seem to have anything to live for. Her husband had left for the US well before I was born and had died there. Her main responsibility was to look after me, and I didn't seem worth staying alive for. There was hardly any affection or attention coming from her, and I soon became a burden for her. She was terminally ill and mainly focused on her illness. She had little time for me and prayed daily to her gods for her life. I remember watching her one day and thinking "What a waste of time and how useless it is to pray to these gods. If you know you have little time left, why not spend it as happily as possible, like playing with your grandchild?" Grandmother finally died when I was 3-1/2.

At her funeral, I felt nothing but outrage over her body being displayed in a propped-up, open casket. And I told them I thought this was undignified. I shocked my aunt by telling her to stop crying because Grandmother's suffering had ended and she was finally at peace. Afterward, sadly, I had to leave my wonderful house, and eventually my village and all my friends. During this time, things and events became a blur, involving staying at different people's homes and traveling with my aunt and later an uncle who brought me all the way to Hong Kong to live with some well-to-do distant relatives by the time I was 4-1/2. The couple had two grown sons and two daughters, one of whom was around my age. I did not feel welcome there. But they did begrudgingly feed and shelter me. I was to spend the next 1-1/2 years in this household until it was time to join my parents in the US when I turned 6. I remember Hong Kong being a wonderful place in which to be a child, and I was happy and comfortable there. I spent a lot of time with the servant and her little son, which proved to be an excellent arrangement for all involved.

Then came the day I was to leave Hong Kong to join my parents in the US. I was excited to be boarding a plane for the first time in my life on Pan Am, dubbed "the world's most experienced airline." On board sitting next to me was an elderly lady who was asked by my parents to keep an eye on me during the flight. There was actually very little for her to do. The stewardesses doted on me and took very good care of me. One even gave me a stewardess pin and brought me to a play area on the plane. It was a long flight with a stopover in Honolulu, Hawaii. I remember the whole experience as being comfortable and pleasant. Upon arrival in San Francisco, my parents were there to pick me up. This was when I found out for the first time that I had a 3-year-old sister. Straight away, my mother gifts the elderly woman a gold bracelet for watching over me. I thought that her simply breathing and sitting next to me on the plane did not warrant a gold bracelet. I was no trouble at all, being this quiet, adorable, and well-behaved little girl that the stewardesses fussed over. Later, Mother would blame me for costing her a gold bracelet (obviously, I wasn't worth it) along with other insults, such as picking up the wrong child at the airport, echoed by Father. Mother also said, "Look how hideous you are compared to me and your little sister (I was tanned from the Hong Kong sun); you couldn't possibly belong to this family." They said this so many times, I started to believe it to be true—that I was an orphan they had to put up with and that they were actually my foster parents.

I lived in shock, desperation, and despair for most of my first year with my parents in the US. After that, I settled in and got used to the abuse, knowing I just had to find a way to survive this. I landed in a very hostile environment where I was all alone, unprotected, and scared, with no friends or allies. There was no refuge, no one to talk to, and no one on my side. I was left to my own devices. I saw myself as a well-behaved and obedient little girl who did nothing wrong. But to Mother, everything I did was wrong and punishable. I loved Mother and did everything I could to please her, but the message coming from her was that I could do nothing right and everything was my fault.

I washed dishes, cleaned the house, and babysat my little sister. Mother never praised or encouraged me or touched me except to beat me. Beatings were her expression of love, or so she had me believe. Therefore, the harder the beatings, the more intense her love.

Scenes From a Childhood

Shortly after arriving in the States, I awoke from an afternoon nap and told Mother how happy I was to be home at last. I did not feel welcome and safe in Hong Kong with those relatives. Without a word, she goes into the closet, pulls out a large square cloth, and wraps my clothes in it. Then she hands me the bundle and tells me she never wants to see me again. She orders me to leave and never return. I do not remember exactly what I did or felt at that very moment. I ran the whole gamut of feelings from numbness to shock to helplessness to terror. And I so much wanted to fulfill her wish. I would have done so if I were in my village, where I was always welcome and safe. But for here and now, this was not an option. I am at her mercy and totally dependent on her for my survival, a fact I deeply resented. Below are some incidents during my first year in the US.

It is my first Christmas. I go downtown with my mother and sister to see Santa Claus in a department store to have our picture taken sitting on his lap. Mother is reluctant to do so because her scratches are visible on my face and visible in the photo.

I am standing at the kitchen stove as tears run down in rivulets. I am sobbing uncontrollably and choking and feeling so hurt. Father says they made a big mistake at the airport, and I cannot possibly be their child. Mother says, "I think you're hurting her feelings." Father replies, "That's impossible; she has no feelings."

I am six years old and proud to be able to get myself up in the mornings, wash and dress myself, make breakfast, and walk myself a couple of blocks to school while Mother continues sleeping. I am about to leave the flat when she awakes to inspect my outfit—a lovely pleated plaid green skirt, white blouse, and a solid orange wool cardigan. I thought I looked great, but she proceeds to beat me because the colors don't match. I end up having to change my outfit and crying all the way to school.

I am alone in the bathtub, enjoying making air balloons with my washcloth by pulling it underwater like a submarine. Nearby, my mother is quietly observing me. She decides now is a good time to push my head underwater and hold me down as if to drown me. I thought today might be my last day on Earth.

I am having dinner with Mother and Sister. Out of the blue, Mother accuses me of picking out the best pieces of meat and vegetables. I honestly have no idea what she's talking about. I only took whatever pieces that were the nearest. This bad behavior called for yet another beating.

Having just arrived in June and knowing no English, I had to learn the alphabet before entering first grade in September. Mother helps me learn as quickly as possible by beating me and keeping me up all night until I can spell words like "apple" and "baby" correctly. It looked as though she and Grandmother share the same teaching method. All I learned from these experiences was that learning equals pain, shame, and torture.

Mother takes me shopping for school supplies. I choose a pencil box that should do the trick. She picks another fancier and more expensive one and asks me if I wouldn't like this one as well. She does a good job selling it to me, pointing out some special features and succeeds in convincing me to take this one as well, although I don't really need or want it. Back home, she berates me for my greediness and my costing her too much money.

My first year in elementary school was a living hell. My first-grade teacher, a fat black lady, was taking out her anger and frustration over whatever inequities she might have endured by constantly humiliating me in front of my class, thereby giving my classmates license to bully me. I would often find my coat on the floor of the cloakroom trampled on and my lunch was stolen daily. At first, I thought Mother was punishing me by giving me only milk for lunch. One day, I found only a few grapes in my very pretty, but mostly empty, lunchbox.

That's when it dawned on me that my lunch was being stolen on a daily basis. I did not dare tell Mother because I knew it would not end well. It was much easier to simply go hungry.

A boy from my class rushes up to me on the street corner on my way home from school, plants a slobbering kiss on my mouth, and then runs away. This felt like a sexual assault. In this kiss, I felt all the contempt of my first-grade class. In the beginning, I wanted to tell Mother all about my experiences in school, both good and bad, but she wasted no time in telling me she had no interest in my drivel and to stop talking to her.

Mother and I are on the street. She says I forgot something and makes me return home alone a couple of blocks away to retrieve it. I am crying and so upset because I am unable to get the door open. A man sees me in distress and comes to help me get the door open. Later, Mother scolds me for allowing this man to help me because he might have made an imprint of the key, thereby compromising our security.

Mother orders me to return something we borrowed from a lady. I know the neighborhood but cannot remember the house. She stands there on the street watching me search frantically for what feels like an eternity before she finally tells me where to go.

One day, during open house at my school, Father shows up while class is in progress. My only thought was this cannot be good. He approaches my first-grade teacher who proceeds to air all her grievances about me. He listens, nods this wise nod (an expression I have never seen and would never see again), and practically proclaims in front of my whole class, "Yes, but that's perfectly normal. You see, she has no brain." At that moment, I imagined the Earth opening up and swallowing me whole. I thought I would die from humiliation.

I board a crowded bus. A man gropes me between my legs. To get away, I took my sister's hand and simply got off at the next stop. I always thought I would be protected from such advances because, according to Mother, I was supposed to be so ugly. I do not tell Mother about this incident because she would not be able to handle it. Everything relating to sex is dirty to her and is something she doesn't do or know how to deal with, except maybe with her lover years later.

My parents want to go out for the evening. They want me to babysit my 3-year-old sister. Mother asks me if I am afraid to stay home alone. I tell her no. She keeps asking me if I am sure that I am not afraid to the point where she starts to scare me. I admit that now I am a bit afraid. She is angry that I spoiled her evening, and they now have to give up their plans and stay home with us. This situation did not last long. Very shortly after, they had no trouble leaving me home alone with my sister. I remember one night the fire department rang our doorbell and told us to evacuate the building because of a small fire. I calmly led my sister out of the building onto the street in our pajamas. I later told my parents about this incident, but they didn't seem concerned.

The men in my family were more or less invisible. I never heard my mother or my father talk about their fathers. Yet, in the dining room hung the pictures of my paternal grandfather and maternal grandmother (one of the first doctors of Western medicine in China). I never met either of them, and I had no relationship with my own father, either. He worked as a waiter at Trader Vic's, came home late, got up late, and sat silently smoking on the living room sofa. He looked unhappy. He rarely talked to me and, at best, merely tolerated me. One of my few memories of him was once waiting with him in a dingy little store in Chinatown in summer, waiting for the delivery of some Chinese dessert made from agar-agar. And there was the time when he took me to see a Chinese opera star who practiced Chinese medicine on the side when, at age 11, I fell and hurt my arm. Father hurt me more by the way he applied pressure in rubbing the medicine into my arm.

Mother is invited to a garden party. She takes me and my sister along. I am dressed in a silly frilly dress that is uncomfortable and hard to play in. There are a lot of children running around and playing. A little girl carrying a Coke runs into me, spilling the Coke onto my dress. Back home, Mother is so upset that she pushes me out in the street, not allowing me to come into the house. It is cold out, and it is embarrassing to stand out there in this ridiculous outfit.

My parents have a huge fight. They proceed to trash the dining room by throwing things all over the place. There is a huge mess with broken dishes, spilled liquids, and rice gruel mixed with the soil of potted plants. Afterward, they both angrily storm out of the house. I clean up the awful mess because I do not want to deal with yet another adult tantrum. My vision starts deteriorating from the ongoing trauma and stress and the things I simply do not want to see—like my mother's accusations, rage, and hatred. I need stronger and stronger glasses. I do not do well in school because practically everybody needs to continuously convince me I'm dumb and hopeless, and that all learning is in vain. I keep wondering what they can possibly gain from my failing. Is there something about me that threatens them so much that it needs to be crushed?

I find myself mostly clueless about the alleged wrongdoing I'm being punished for, but I often find myself being pushed into a locked dark storage room, out onto the street, or out onto the cold stairwell as punishment. We live on the fourth floor, and each apartment has its own private staircase.

Sister finds a jar of macadamia nuts in the cupboard and proceeds to consume the whole jar. Mother is furious that I had allowed this to happen. In a hysterical fit, she proceeds to trash the dining room, throwing everything out of the cupboard onto the floor. Some jars break and glass shatters. There is a mess of foodstuff all over the floor. When she's done, she goes to bed. I stand there paralyzed, not knowing what I should do. I don't dare go to bed because I don't think it's safe to do so. By 3:00 am, she finally comes back in to order me to go to bed.

Mother had endearing names for me, her favorites being "moron" and "pig." I am constantly reminded by both my parents and teachers throughout elementary school how stupid, useless, and hopeless I am, that I would never amount to anything in life, and that there was no point in even trying. I developed a ducking reflex whenever Mother made a sudden swift movement because I expected to be hit or slapped. She didn't spare the rod, either.

Mother suddenly feels the need to punish me for what I don't know. I think she needs to relieve tension. She takes a large crate of oranges and proceeds to cut them all open. She forces me to eat and eat until it tastes bitter, and I vomit it all over the kitchen floor. She is not impressed. She continues to force-feed me the oranges.

The female neighbor, a friend of hers, enters through the kitchen and steps right into my vomit. She acts as if this were nothing out of the ordinary. I am crying, eating oranges, while Mother continues to cut them open for me. Our neighbor says she sees that we're busy and that she will come back later. I am being tortured by a madwoman, and both adults act as if this were normal behavior instead of the child abuse that it is.

Everything described above is from age six during my first year in San Francisco, being reunited with my parents. I knew that if I could successfully survive this first year, I would be able to bear whatever happens thereafter. I don't remember a moment when I thought I was unlovable, at fault, or a bad person. I did not take on my mother's point of view, values, unhappiness, shame, need to conform, or to look good. She regarded me as undifferentiated from her, as part of her, and as "her property," as she once told me. I was present to all—the pain, the terror, and the abuse—and dealt with it as best I could. I did not dissociate. I knew it would eventually end, but for now, I just needed to safeguard my sanity and endure. I was still a mostly happy and carefree child.

I did love my mother and tried in vain to please her. But it seemed as if I could never do anything right. She was beautiful, talented, resilient, and resourceful. She was a fantastic cook and top-notch tailor, preparing delicious and nutritious meals and sewing a lot of clothes for my sister and me. She studied hard to pass a difficult exam to become a hairdresser to support my sister and me after she divorced her abusive husband when I was around 12. She and I could have had a wonderful mother-daughter relationship. I needed a mother and a role model, not a rival, narcissist, and conformist. I needed her love, support, and guidance, and I could have learned so much from her. This lost opportunity is something I will always regret. I think I might have overdone it in differentiating from her. Sometimes it was easier for me to think of her as mentally ill than to think of her as not loving and wanting me. I thought that even if she didn't love me, she could at least be kind.

China and America were two very different experiences. In the former, I felt unconditionally loved; I was significant, accepted, respected, supported, protected, and even celebrated. These first years in China insulated me from later mistreatment and trauma. Mother once told me she heard wonderful things about me from relatives in China. It sounded as if she were talking about someone who died. "What happened to you?" she would ask. And I wanted to answer: "You happened to me." Around my parents, I mostly felt like an unwelcome and unwarranted burden at best. At worst, I was despised as someone stupid, ugly, worthless, hopeless, and undeserving of love, attention, support, protection, and guidance. I was someone who was continually humiliated, insulted, and gaslighted, as well as physically, mentally, and emotionally abused. It felt like practically everything I did was either deemed bad or wrong, where I was left to my own devices, forever confused as to what was the right way or right thing to do. The message I got from this environment was that I was unlovable, I cost too much, I was undeserving, not worth it, and an inconvenience. The only problem was I didn't buy it.

Many years later, when I brought up the subject of her cruel treatment towards me, both she and my sister denied such things had ever happened and claimed I had made the whole thing up. In the end, she did concede with this puzzling statement: "I understand; I too was once young." Ultimately, nothing she said mattered; I never needed an apology.

As a result of my first years in China, I was sufficiently differentiated from my parents in that I did not share their views, values, or opinions of me. I never actually believed what my parents and teachers said about me. I never thought I was unlovable just because my parents didn't love me. They could even be commended for being honest and not pretending to feel something for me they didn't feel. I knew I was a good, kind, pretty, happy, and lovable child, no matter what anyone said or thought about me. I simply did not accept their opinions. I helped Mother by doing household chores and babysitting my sister from age six on. I washed, cleaned, shopped, and even cooked when she was at school or working. I was a boring teenager: I never rebelled, dated, partied, or gave them any reason to worry or feel ashamed. Mother felt shame anyway because she had this strong need to conform and fit in. But I did not share her shame, nor did I take on the shame she might have felt for the way she treated me. She was forever invading my privacy and my boundaries by searching through my stuff hoping to find whatever secrets I might be hiding from her. Aha, gotcha—embroidery and novels! She never did find out (or maybe pretended not to know) about her lover's secret of fondling me while I slept (I was 13 by then). I kept quiet about this to be spared her hysterics and attacks.

Beneath it all, I was this happy, carefree, innocent child who believed in the good in people. What saved me and solaced me were those first few years spent in China, where my identity and character were forged and where there was this deep inner conviction, integrity, and internal bliss that the highs and lows of life could not impact. In the end, it mattered little to me whether people loved me or not, and their bullying did not faze me either. I often saw it as their problem and their unhappiness, for which I was not responsible. Looking back, I can see that I was able to put up with a lot. I never held a grudge. I never envied anyone or wished I were someone else. I admit to thinking it unfair that my little sister got all the parental love and attention, and I did fantasize about being somewhere else and belonging to a loving family. Although I easily forgave everyone for everything done to me, my self-esteem and confidence did take a beating in this hostile environment. I often felt alone, helpless, and invisible. I thought people behaved badly because they were hurting or unhappy or unloved or ignorant.

I think Mother was full of anger. She felt robbed of a carefree childhood because of war; she married beneath her station, and then was compelled to leave China. She came from wealth and privilege and now had to struggle to make a living. This was not what she signed up for. And she was just not cut out to be my mother. I understood her and felt bad for her. But this does not justify her treatment of me. Although I am grateful to her for giving me life, she never chose to have me. She resented my very existence and took her unhappiness out on me. I felt deprived of loving parents and a safe environment to grow up in. I felt despised and yet engulfed by my mother, who resented anything or anybody who took my attention away from her. She did not like seeing me happy and preoccupied only with myself. My sister was the smart, beautiful, and talented one deserving of Mother's love. I loved my sister and was happy she was treated well. But I also know that the sibling who witnesses the abuse is the one who ends up the more traumatized. I left home for good by the time I was 20 and never looked back. My sister is still there.

I cannot remember a single time my parents ever praised me or showed me affection, encouragement, or approval. Probably the happiest day of my time in elementary school was when my sixth-grade male teacher gave me a speech to deliver to kick off the graduation ceremony. I memorized the speech and delivered it impeccably, crisp and clear, without the need for a microphone. My teacher was very satisfied and proud of me, as was I. All my classmates were being showered with affection by their parents. It appeared that the only people missing from this happy occasion were both my parents. But this was of no consequence, and it did little to dampen my spirits. By then, they had both ceased to be of any significance.

What I learned about love is that I am enough, and I am lovable no matter what others may say or think about me. They are entitled to their feelings and opinions, which do not concern me or define me. There is what happened to me, what I got or didn't get, and my interpretation of what happened. That interpretation is a choice, and I choose to have come out of it unscathed--the victor vs. the victim. The only opinions that matter are the ones that are uplifting, empowering, liberating, and the ones I want to be true about me. If none exists, then I'll just have to make them up.

Chapter 3:

What Others Say

I posed this question to a number of people (and roughly half of them responded):

"What would a love that sets you free mean to you—what would it look like, feel like, how would your life be impacted, what would it make possible for you that isn't possible now?"

Katherine

A love that sets me free means I am encouraged, supported, nurtured into coming into my own, where my dreams, gifts, talents, and passions are respected and taken seriously.

As a small child, I remember my mom inventing stories with me and encouraging me to invent my own stories and adventures with my toys. She also read me stories and told me stories she made up and, at some point, I joined her. I remember my stay-at-home mom always being busy with household chores, but she always made time to invent stories with or for me. She was good at playing different roles and doing different voices.

My mom was also an avid reader and, through her, I discovered my love for books. As a result, reading, writing, and inventing came easily to me, and I continued to tell my mom made-up stories. She found them funny and entertaining and encouraged me to write them down, which I did.

My mom encouraged and nurtured my creativity and, without knowing it, she showed me a way to my freedom, to come into my own, as an expression of her love. And basically, that's how I easily came into my chosen profession as an actress and a theater workshop leader, creating a free space where people feel safe to explore, imagine, and try out things with others and for themselves.

Betty

The love that sets me free is the genuine love I have inside myself from the beginning of my life until the end.

It is a love I have to discover every day again and again; a love that makes me think big, and lets me transcend fears that are often subtle and unseen, but which nevertheless have a great impact on my life.

The love that sets me free is bigger than me and sometimes frightening because it shows me my power and the possibilities for my life.

The love that sets me free is like a big mother believing in me more than I do, opening a new world for me every day.

Sam

The love that sets me free is the unconditional love of myself: to love myself with all of my utterly irrational desires, flaws, weaknesses, and shortcomings.

It means to love myself in all my pettiness and all my greatness, as if I were my own child, with compassion and indulgence. It requires me to value and trust in this love more than I value and trust in the love of anybody else.

Amy

For me, the most difficult and longest lesson was simply learning to love and accept myself exactly as I am. To find out I am not only "good" and "decent," but also that I can be very bitchy at times, and that this—the light and dark sides of me—is all part of who I am, was empowering.

In the last few years, I really learned and experienced how it felt to be really proud of myself when I started a job that fit me 100%. My job also leveraged my dark sides, as it was sometimes necessary to be assertive, forceful, and demanding in order to achieve things for the 1,500 people I was responsible for. I'm proud about having produced and raised a beautiful little daughter and, with all the things I have on my plate, to still be a caring daughter for my 89-year-old parents. And I know I can handle all of this because it makes me happy. I simply love my life, and I finally experience total self-love and self-acceptance after all these years. One part I have not integrated as well into my life is the part where I am less dependent on the love and approval of others. But the fact that I am aware of this is already something I am proud of.

Hanna

My thoughts for a love that sets me free are as follows: The first problem is the expression to "fall" in love, rather than to "rise" in love.

If we fall, it might hurt. If we rise, we can raise and spread our wings above all. Most people also fall in love with what they think or expect love to be: the thrill, the excitement, the honeymoon, and so on, instead of dealing with another human being not unlike themselves. We encounter the toxic experience of love when we focus on what we expect love to give us—sexual pleasure, security, infatuation, and freedom from loneliness, so often combined with fear of abandonment, loss, or death.

My very personal experience has to do with what we call God. My own longing to experience the essence of myself—the being, the feelings—was for a long time focused on men, and the result was separation, regrets, and unhappiness.

We have been given free will to explore, to accept, to deny, and to experience.

The love that now sets me free is the exciting process with the ups and downs of life itself, the love of the Invisible Source, or living God, the Light that affords me the power to help and heal others. It has been a long but deeply fulfilling and worthwhile journey getting there.

Piers

Love rarely sets anyone free. Because it means you will be connected to someone or something which would then involve compromises. No love can continue without that, because it would be one-sided and dictatorial. The compromises could water down freedom of movement, thought, dreams, and desires.

Matthew

A "love that sets me free" would have me waking up in the morning with anticipation and curiosity about a day full of opportunities to make a contribution to life. I would be full of joy for what I am capable of creating and fulfilling. I would fall asleep in the evening full of pride for what I had accomplished that day. I would be full of gratitude for all that I have, for what others have done for me, and for what I was able to contribute and experience that day. In the absence of that, I would miss the feeling of being enough and the satisfaction of knowing I had given my all toward what is important to me.

Paolo

The love that sets one free can really never be human love... we're too selfish and self-centered. There are different kinds of love: erotic love, filial love, and agape love. A husband and wife, or lovers, experience erotic love. Filial love is that of a child or parent, or "brotherly" love.

Both are very powerful forms of love, but not necessarily freeing. Erotic love for obvious reasons... more often than not, we want to satisfy our partner, but at the same time, be satisfied. Jealousy can creep in. Filial love is similar in the sense that the love we have for children, parents, or great friends often revolves around a give-and-take in the relationship. For example, we love our children, but we want to be loved in return.

Agape love, on the other hand, is unmerited, gracious, and constantly seeking the good of the other, for the other's sake. It is truly unselfish, with no regard or thought of how it affects us the giver. In my humble opinion, this kind of love is the only one that can set us free. Yet, as human beings, we cannot give this kind of love. It can only be generated from the divine, and we are free only when we acknowledge that and accept it.

Tina

For me, it means to care and be interested in one another's total well-being—spiritually, mentally, and physically. It means knowing and feeling cherished just as I am, and believing that I am enough at this very moment, with no restrictions, expectations, or judgment. It also means being eager to share happiness, wanting for the other to be successful in all their endeavors, listening attentively, encouraging one another, and sharing thoughts and feelings. A love that sets one free also requires an alignment of vision for the future, discussing and communicating openly while appreciating and respecting one another's vulnerability with honesty and sincerity.

Desiree

The word "love" has a multitude of meanings to us humans. We love one another, love our spouse, children, parents, and siblings, love a good book, cool breezes, fishing, baseball, old movies, and so on. It is a noun, a verb, an emotion, a feeling, and a state of mind.

Love, in its most liberating and empowering form, is an experience that transcends the superficial confines of romantic partnerships or familial bonds. It is an unwavering force of acceptance, understanding, and growth, offering each individual the freedom to be their authentic self. This love ignites a sense of empowerment, enabling one to embrace their unique identity and embark on a journey of self-discovery.

A love that sets me free is one that is non-judgmental and fosters an environment where vulnerability is cherished. It encourages open communication and the sharing of thoughts, feelings, and experiences without fear of rejection or ridicule. This type of love is grounded in the mutual recognition of each other's humanity, allowing for growth and learning from one another's differences. When love is truly liberating, it provides a solid foundation for personal and collective healing.

This love cultivates a safe space where individuals can navigate through past traumas, confront emotional pain, and work toward inner peace. By embracing the transformative power of love, we can break free from self-imposed limitations and reach our full potential.

In essence, a love that sets us free is one that nurtures our deepest emotional and spiritual needs. It is a love that encourages us to explore our inner landscapes, without fearing judgment or isolation. This empowering, liberating, and healing love is not only a gift to ourselves, but also a beacon of hope and inspiration for those around us. It is the wind beneath our wings.

Janet

The love I have with my son is what keeps me going. We have always had a strong connection. We are so attuned to each other. If it's midnight and he texts me, I am immediately aware of it. I pick him up and he does the same for me.

When I was in the hospital, he tried to paint my fingernails. It was a disaster, but it meant so much. He brings me small gifts, calls me Mama, and tells me he loves me all the time. I feel incredibly blessed. What more could I ask for?

Jenna

The love that sets you free means the following to me:

- when you accept those who meet you where you are at
- when you allow those to imperfectly but consistently encourage you
- when you share intimacy in a touch, a look, in words, in your history
- when you know what you need to be happy and that is supported
- when you do all this work on yourself and give it back in return
- and when you learn how to walk away from those who don't

Christine

A love that sets you free would mean to love myself. I am free when I trust that all the love I need is within. Through this love, I know my self worth, feel confident, and can meet all people with loving kindness.

Theresia

"You well know that the one who loves does not feel the hardship" (St. Francis de Assisi quotes, n.d.).

This quotation from St. Francis de Assisi speaks to me. From experience, I know that sometimes it means hardship to love. I love both my daughters unconditionally. The older one, however, keeps me at bay and is barely communicating with me for reasons she won't disclose. It tears at my heart, but I will keep on loving her deeply. I will not see it as a hardship or struggle any longer to be pushed back. Rather, I'm grateful for the gift to be able to love, and will continue to love her and all those close to me.

Tanya

Growing up, I weathered storms of self-doubt and endured the cutting remarks of those who failed to see my worth.

One poignant chapter unfolded when, at the tender age of 12, my mom's illness swept my world, placing me under the care of an aunt for two long years. However, this phase wasn't just marked by familial shifts—it held the haunting presence of my cousin's boyfriend, who cast a dark shadow over my days.

In the clandestine corners of our shared space, he subjected me to a cruel dance of emotional and physical abuse. An unrelenting storm of torment, I faced emotional neglect, feeling like a phantom—an "extra unbelonged." Their cat basked in the warmth of love, while I dwelled in the chilling shadows of blame, made to feel like an intruder merely for existing and taking space. Yet, with the passing seasons, and over many years, I refused to let these wounds define me.

In the serene gardens of my mind, I cultivated a sanctuary. With each whispered word of kindness, I watered the soil, drowning the weeds of self-doubt with the nourishing elixir of self-love. Today, those words have become seeds—a vibrant garden of confidence, resilience, and self-belief. To nurture this sacred space, I've embraced the magic of self-talk, understanding that even one beautiful word can wield tremendous power.

In this enchanting garden, I've sown seeds of:

- grace
- courage
- gratitude
- serenity
- resilience
- harmony
- abundance
- empowerment
- peace
- joy
- optimism
- compassion
- strength
- wisdom
- hope
- creativity

These words, like petals in a breeze, carry the fragrance of my resilience. They've transformed the narrative, allowing me to dance freely to the melody of my own existence. The importance of nurturing our inner gardens cannot be overstated. Neglecting this sacred space can breed weeds of despair. I've learned, through empowering experiences, that it's vital to be happy, to let go of the shadows of the past, and to speak words that breathe life into our spirits. In the quiet whispers of self-love, in the embrace of those who see our worth, lies the key to a garden that blooms with the hues of our truest selves. Let's tend to these gardens with care, for they hold the power to transform our stories into sagas of resilience, beauty, and unyielding self-love. In the corridors of memory, my aunt, a figure both narcissistic and wicked, still lingers like the infamous "Baba Yaga" from Russian folk tales—a hag who despised children, relished baking them into treats, and soared on a broomstick with a malevolent nose and evil eyes. Although forgiveness has softened the edges of resentment over the years, the image endures. A professor of mathematics in a Siberian university of heating, she wove a tapestry of disdain, declaring me "uneducable" and prophesying a bleak future for my brother and me—mine in the shadows of a low-grade school for "nobodies" or a brothel house, and my brother destined for the chaos of a war zone, doomed to insignificance.

Yet, life painted a different canvas. My brother claimed the first chair in the woodwind orchestra, a laureate of international acclaim with his clarinet talent. As for me, a person adorned with myriad talents in the performing and visual arts, I've embraced everything life has to offer, including unlimited and unconditional love with my loving husband and two most precious beautiful children, reclaiming a narrative that defies the grim prophecies of yesteryears.

Ray

From my perspective and in my world view, there exists the relative and the absolute domain. Love in the relative domain is conditional, and only in the absolute domain is love unconditional. Therefore, to try and love unconditionally in the relative domain is to set oneself up for entanglement in codependency at best, and total abuse at worst.

In fact, whenever we expect ourselves to give, or others to receive unconditional love, we are confusing conditional with unconditional love. This is because expectations exist only in the relative domain. In the absolute domain, there are no expectations because when we are in touch with it, we experience unconditional love and absolute freedom. We don't need to give or receive it, because we are it.

Therefore, when we open up to a direct experience of the absolute domain, it is obvious that only unconditional love sets you free. However, although we are all born with the potential to open up to the absolute domain, and to experience unconditional love and absolute freedom, most of us don't even come close to consciously experiencing them, as we tend to identify with our relative identity—namely, our physical body-mind and our subtle body-mind, as well as our emotions, feelings, thoughts, and convictions.

Although every day we move from being awake to dreaming in sleep to dreamless sleep, and from gross to subtle to causal reality. In those "peak experiences," we get a taste of unconditional love and absolute freedom.

These experiences usually don't last very long, and soon we find ourselves contracted into our small body-mind identity in gross reality. However, with practice, we can learn to open up and stabilize our access to subtle and causal states, slowly losing our attachments to conditional love and freedom, thereby shifting the center of gravity of our identity from gross to subtle and causal.

If we temporarily succeed in shifting our center of gravity into the causal state, we still have physical and subtle bodies. We still experience pain and joy, only more deeply, profoundly, and meaningfully. Even if only for short periods of time, we begin to experience unconditional love and absolute freedom. The more we succeed in expanding our awareness, the more we can differentiate between conditional and unconditional love, relative and absolute freedom. This begins to impact all our relationships with people, nature, and all of reality.

As a result, we begin to understand the paradox that, in the relative domain, "unconditional love cannot be given unconditionally," which allows us to transcend the entanglements of co-dependent relationships and sets us free.

We can let go of instinctive impulses to dominate and control others, nature, and reality, just to feel safe. We learn to relax more and more into what Pema Chödrön called the "groundlessness of our own existence" (Pema Chödrön quotes, n.d.).

Hayley

The simplest interactions of love—such as a shared smile, a spontaneous hug, a mutual laugh, or a knowing glance—warm my heart and wash over me with joy.

Marie

To me, love is the most important feeling in life.

Whoever doesn't know this, or doesn't feel its life-giving vibrations, is emotionally numb.

Love is simply the joy of seeing and experiencing the world as it is.

It could be the simple pleasure of seeing a field, enjoying fresh air, colorful flowers, nature in all its glory. Or, it could be found through family, hugging friends, or seeing smiling faces full of joy.

PART 2
Barriers to Love

Chapter 4:

Patriarchy's Influence on Love

Patriarchy's Impact on Women

Patriarchy is a social system in which men hold primary power and predominate in roles of political leadership, moral authority, social privilege, and control of property. Its impact on women has been profound and continues to manifest in various ways, though it is essential to note that the impact can vary across different cultures and historical periods. Some of the key impacts of patriarchy on women include:

- **Gender Inequality:** Patriarchy reinforces and perpetuates gender inequality by granting men more power and privileges than women in various aspects of life, such as politics, economics, and decision-making.

- **Limited Access to Education and Economic Opportunities:** In patriarchal societies, women may have limited access to education and employment opportunities, which can hinder their personal and economic development.

- **Gender Pay Gap:** Patriarchal norms often contribute to a gender pay gap, where women earn less than men for similar work, which can have long-term economic consequences.

- **Gender-based Violence:** Patriarchy can contribute to a culture of violence against women, including domestic violence, sexual harassment, and assault. Women may be less likely to report such incidents due to societal norms that dismiss or downplay their experiences.

- **Restricted Reproductive Rights:** In some patriarchal societies, women's reproductive rights may be restricted, including access to contraception and abortion, which can affect their control over their own bodies and family planning.

- **Limitations on Political Participation:** Patriarchy can limit women's participation in politics and decision-making processes, leading to under-representation in positions of power and influence.

- **Stereotyping and Objectification:** Women are often stereotyped and objectified in patriarchal societies, which can reduce their agency and opportunities, as well as reinforce harmful beauty standards.

- **Pressure to Conform to Gender Roles:** Patriarchy enforces rigid gender roles, with women expected to fulfill specific domestic and caregiving roles, limiting their freedom to pursue other aspirations.

- **Emotional and Psychological Impact:** The constant exposure to gender discrimination and stereotypes can take a toll on women's mental and emotional well-being, leading to stress, anxiety, and depression.

- **Limitations on Personal Autonomy:** Women may have fewer choices regarding their personal lives, such as whom to marry, when to have children, or how to express their sexuality.

- **Reduced Access to Healthcare:** In some societies, women may have limited access to healthcare, including reproductive and maternal healthcare, which can have severe health consequences.

- **Cultural and Social Stigmatization:** Women who challenge patriarchal norms and attempt to assert their rights may face social stigma, discrimination, and backlash.

- **Low Expectations of Them:** Women are often encouraged to "marry well" and be taken care of. Their dreams, talents, and ambitions may not be supported or tolerated.

Addressing these challenges requires a multi-faceted approach involving policy changes, legal protections, education and awareness, and the active involvement of both men and women. By challenging gender norms, promoting equal opportunities, and working towards dismantling systemic barriers, we can strive towards a more inclusive and equitable society that empowers women to fulfill their potential and live free from discrimination and violence.

Patriarchy's Impact on Men

The greatest challenge facing men today is the evolving definition of masculinity and the pressures associated with it. For centuries, society has held certain expectations of men, emphasizing traits such as strength, dominance, and emotional stoicism. However, in recent years, these traditional notions of masculinity have come under scrutiny, challenging men to redefine their roles.

Patriarchy not only affects women but also has an impact on men. While men typically benefit from the privileges associated with patriarchal systems, there are also negative consequences for men that result from these structures. It is important to recognize that the impact of patriarchy on men can vary depending on cultural, social, and individual factors. Here are some of the ways in which patriarchy can affect men:

- **Gender Roles and Expectations:** Patriarchy enforces rigid gender roles, pressuring men to conform to traditional notions of masculinity. Men are often expected to be strong, unemotional, and the primary providers, which can limit their emotional expression and personal choices.

- **Emotional Suppression:** Patriarchal norms discourage men from expressing vulnerability or emotions beyond anger. This emotional suppression can lead to mental health issues and difficulties in forming meaningful relationships.

- **Pressure to Succeed:** Men may experience intense pressure to succeed in their careers and social lives, as their worth in a patriarchal society is often measured by their achievements and financial success.

- **Competitiveness and Aggression:** Patriarchy can encourage a competitive and aggressive mindset, which may lead to harmful behaviors and conflicts in personal and professional relationships.

- **Limited Expressions of Intimacy:** Men may have fewer opportunities to engage in emotional intimacy and close relationships, as these are sometimes considered "feminine" qualities in patriarchal societies.

- **Fathers and Caregivers:** Patriarchy can limit men's involvement in caregiving roles, including as fathers. The expectation that women should be the primary caregivers can prevent men from fully participating in their children's lives.

- **Reinforcement of Homophobia:** Patriarchy often perpetuates homophobia and rigid gender norms, which can lead to discrimination against LGBTQ+ individuals. This could get in the way of their forging strong male friendships that are supportive, nurturing, and healing.

- **Toxic Masculinity:** The pressure to conform to traditional masculinity norms can lead to toxic masculinity, which promotes behaviors like sexism, dominance, and aggression, often to the detriment of both men and women.

- **Resistance to Seeking Help:** Men may be less likely to seek help for mental health issues or physical health concerns due to social stigmas associated with vulnerability and weakness.

- **Reinforcement of Male Privilege:** While men may face certain negative consequences of patriarchy, they also benefit from the privileges it confers. It's important to acknowledge these privileges and work toward a more equitable society for all.

It is crucial to recognize that many men are actively challenging patriarchal norms and working towards more egalitarian and inclusive societies. Efforts to break free from harmful gender stereotypes and expectations are beneficial not only for women but for men as well, as they allow for greater emotional and personal freedom and healthier, more fulfilling relationships.

Beyond Gender

Both men and women can face various problems and concerns that may be influenced by individual, societal, or cultural factors. These issues can include mental health challenges, relationship problems, career-related stress, and more. It's crucial to treat each person as an individual and not assume that they will experience specific issues based on their gender.

It's important to note that issues related to anger, violence, or any other behavioral or psychological challenges are not exclusive to any gender. People of all genders can experience a wide range of issues and challenges, and it's not appropriate to generalize or stereotype based on gender.

The Impact of Toxic Masculinity on Men and Women

Toxic masculinity refers to a set of socially constructed attitudes, beliefs, and behaviors that are traditionally associated with men and masculinity, but which are harmful to both men and women. It is important to note that toxic masculinity does not imply that all men exhibit toxic behaviors or that masculinity itself is inherently toxic. Rather, it describes the negative effects of rigid societal expectations and stereotypes placed on men, which can have a detrimental impact on romantic relationships.

Toxic masculinity perpetuates harmful gender norms that dictate how men should behave, such as being emotionally stoic, dominant, aggressive, and sexually aggressive. These norms can create a hostile environment for men who do not conform to these expectations and can also negatively affect their relationships with women. Let's explore some ways in which toxic masculinity can affect romantic relationships:

- **Emotional Suppression:** One of the key aspects of toxic masculinity is the suppression of emotions. Men are often taught to hide their feelings, not show vulnerability, and toughen up. In romantic relationships, this emotional suppression can hinder effective communication and emotional intimacy. Men may find it difficult to express their needs, fears, or insecurities, leading to misunderstandings and a lack of emotional connection with their partners.

- **Power Dynamics:** Toxic masculinity promotes power and dominance over others, which can lead to power imbalances in relationships. It may foster a belief that men should always be in control and make all the decisions, undermining the equality and partnership that healthy relationships require. This power dynamic can contribute to relationship conflicts, resentment, and a lack of mutual respect.

- **Aggression and Violence:** Toxic masculinity often associates aggression and violence with strength and control. This can manifest in physical, verbal, or emotional abuse within love relationships. Aggressive behavior becomes a way for men to assert dominance and maintain control, which not only harms their partners but also perpetuates a cycle of violence and toxic behavior.

- **Unrealistic Expectations:** Society places unrealistic expectations on men to conform to certain standards of success, physical appearance, and sexual prowess. Men may feel pressured to be the breadwinners, to have a muscular physique, or to engage in casual sexual encounters. These expectations can lead to anxiety, low self-esteem, and feelings of inadequacy if they do not measure up. In relationships, these pressures can strain the connection, as men may feel inadequate or struggle to meet their partner's expectations.

- **Homophobia and Heteronormativity (strict norms about sexuality as well as strict gender roles within society):** Toxic masculinity reinforces rigid gender roles and stigmatizes anything perceived as "feminine." Men may feel compelled to suppress their true identities and conform to traditional masculine stereotypes, which can limit their ability to explore their own sexuality and establish genuine connections with their partners. This can result in strained relationships, lack of authenticity, and difficulties in communication and establishing emotional and sexual intimacy.

- **Limited Emotional Support:** Toxic masculinity discourages men from seeking emotional support or engaging in self-care practices. This can lead to feelings of isolation and emotional distress, affecting their ability to navigate challenges within relationships effectively. Without a support system or the ability to express emotions openly, men may struggle to address issues in their relationships, leading to unresolved conflicts and resentment.

It is important to recognize that toxic masculinity is not solely a men's issue but a societal issue that affects individuals of all genders. Overcoming toxic masculinity requires collective efforts to challenge and dismantle harmful gender stereotypes and expectations. Here are a couple of strategies to promote healthier romantic relationships:

- **Education and Awareness:** Encourage open discussions and education about toxic masculinity and its impact on relationships. By understanding and recognizing these patterns, individuals can work towards dismantling them and promoting healthier relationship dynamics.

- **Communication and Emotional Intelligence:** Foster an environment of open and honest communication in relationships. Encourage emotional intelligence, where both partners can safely and freely express their feelings.

Furthermore, men are grappling with the shifting dynamics in relationships and dating. With the rise of the #MeToo movement and increased awareness of consent and gender equality, men are re-evaluating their behavior and relearning how to navigate romantic and sexual interactions. The challenge lies in dismantling toxic masculinity and learning healthy ways to express desire, communicate boundaries, and foster mutually respectful relationships.

Additionally, the changing job market and economic pressures present a challenge for men. Traditional industries that once provided stable employment opportunities for men are being disrupted, leading to job insecurity and financial stress. Men are increasingly facing the need to adapt their skills and embrace new industries that require different competencies, which can be challenging and disorienting.

In conclusion, the greatest challenge facing men today is the need to recreate and redefine masculinity and navigate the changing societal expectations. This involves finding a balance between traditional and progressive ideals, addressing mental health issues, embracing healthier relationship dynamics, and adapting to a transforming job market. By acknowledging and actively working towards these challenges, men can contribute to a more inclusive and equitable society that values the diversity of masculinity and promotes the well-being of all individuals. Sometimes "dealing with it like a man" could mean simply having the courage to see what's actually there instead of running away from it. It could mean dropping the mask of masculinity to embrace authenticity and vulnerability.

Chapter 5:

Romantic Love

Love is a fire. But whether it is going to warm your heart or burn down your house, you can never tell. –Joan Crawford

***

Romantic love is a dance of two souls entwined in an intricate choreography of us. It can be a catalyst for personal growth and self-discovery as we embrace the journey that unfolds in unpredictable ways rather than being fixated on a specific destination. And it is not without its problems. In this chapter, I will briefly explore some of the challenges and issues that can arise in the realm of romantic love.

One of the primary problems with romantic love is its transitory nature. Love can be an intense and intoxicating emotion, but it often fades over time. The initial excitement and infatuation that accompanies the early stages of a relationship may give way to a more stable and mature form of love, but it can also lead to disillusionment and disappointment. The passionate flames of love may dwindle, leaving individuals to question their feelings and the sustainability of the relationship.

Another problem with romantic love is its potential to blind people to reality. When we are in love, we tend to idealize our partners and overlook their flaws. This can lead to unrealistic expectations and disappointment when our partners inevitably fall short of the perfect image we have created in our minds. Love can make us ignore red flags or tolerate unhealthy behaviors, jeopardizing our own well-being in the process.

Jealousy and possessiveness are also common issues in romantic relationships. Love can breed insecurity, leading to feelings of possessiveness and a desire to control the actions and interactions of our partners.

This possessive behavior can erode trust and create a toxic dynamic within the relationship. Jealousy can be destructive, causing conflicts and driving a wedge between individuals who should be supporting and uplifting each other. Furthermore, romantic love can lead to a loss of personal identity. In the pursuit of love, individuals may sacrifice their own dreams, ambitions, and interests, subsuming themselves within the relationship.

This can result in a loss of self-esteem and a lack of fulfillment as personal goals are neglected or abandoned. It is essential to strike a balance between love and personal growth, ensuring that both individuals in a relationship have the freedom to pursue their own aspirations while also nurturing their connection.

Romantic love can create an intense fear of rejection or abandonment. The vulnerability that comes with opening oneself up to love can be terrifying. The fear of being hurt or rejected can lead people to build walls and maintain emotional distance, preventing them from fully experiencing the joys and benefits of a loving relationship. Overcoming this fear requires courage, trust, and effective communication between partners.

In conclusion, romantic love is not without its challenges. Its transitory nature, idealization of partners, jealousy, loss of personal identity, and fear of rejection are all issues that can arise. However, acknowledging these problems and actively working on them can help individuals navigate the complexities of romantic relationships and cultivate healthier and more fulfilling connections.

Love requires effort, understanding, and a commitment to personal growth and the growth of the relationship itself. By addressing these challenges, we can strive to build relationships that are not only romantic, but also strong, supportive, and enduring.

The romantic love depicted in movies often presents an idealized and unrealistic version of love that can be misleading and problematic. While movies can be a source of entertainment and inspiration, it's important to recognize the discrepancies between their portrayal of love and the complexities of real-life relationships.

Here are some aspects of romantic love depicted in movies that can be problematic:

- **Unrealistic Expectations**: Movies often depict love as a flawless, effortless, and everlasting experience. They tend to focus on the initial infatuation and the "happily ever after" ending, without delving into the challenges and compromises that real relationships require. This can create unrealistic expectations and leave individuals feeling dissatisfied with their own relationships when they don't live up to these idealized standards.

- **Lack of Communication**: In many movies, conflicts arise from a lack of communication between the romantic partners. Misunderstandings and dramatic plot twists often occur because characters fail to have honest conversations about their feelings and concerns. Real relationships thrive on open and effective communication, which is often glossed over or ignored in movie portrayals.

- **Idealized Characters**: Movie characters are often portrayed as flawless individuals with perfect looks, personalities, and lives. They may possess unrealistic qualities that can make viewers feel inadequate. In reality, people have flaws, insecurities, and make mistakes, and a healthy relationship involves accepting and loving each other despite these imperfections.

- **Focus on Grand Gestures**: Movies often emphasize extravagant displays of love, such as grand romantic gestures or sweeping declarations of affection. While these moments can be emotionally exhilarating, they can overshadow the importance of everyday acts of kindness, respect, and support that sustain a healthy relationship. Real love is built on consistent effort, trust, and mutual respect, rather than solely relying on dramatic displays.

- **Lack of Diversity and Representation**: Movie depictions of romantic love often present a limited scope of relationships, primarily focused on heterosexual, cisgender, and monogamous partnerships. This lack of diversity can contribute to feelings of exclusion and inadequacy among those whose experiences do not align with the depicted norms. It is essential to recognize and celebrate the diversity of love and relationships in real life.

It is crucial to approach movie portrayals of romantic love with a critical eye and an understanding that they are often fictionalized and exaggerated for the purpose of entertainment. Real-life relationships require effort, compromise, and understanding, and they are far more nuanced and complex than what is typically portrayed on the silver screen. Building a healthy and fulfilling relationship involves embracing authenticity, effective communication, mutual respect, and a willingness and resilience to navigate challenges together.

Chapter 6:

Unrequited Love

And there's nothing quite as sad as a one-sided love. When one doesn't care at all and the other cares too much. It's a sad situation, I must say When someone wants to leave as bad as you want them to stay. –Dolly Parton

***

Unrequited love reinforces your feeling of rejection, of being unlovable, not worthy of love, and questioning your worth. It attacks your self-esteem and makes you think love is not available to you. And when you can't have it, it's all that matters.

Unrequited love refers to a situation where one person has romantic feelings for another person who does not reciprocate those feelings. This can happen when the person who is loved does not return the feelings, is not interested in a romantic relationship, or is unaware of the other person's feelings. Unrequited love can be a difficult and painful experience, causing feelings of rejection, loneliness, and heartbreak. It is important for those experiencing unrequited love to take care of their own emotional well-being and to consider seeking support from friends, family, or a mental health professional if needed. One needs to accept that the feelings are not mutual and move on.

Only love people who love you back. You can't make someone love you. As soon as you realize they do not share the same feelings you have for them, you need to be the first to end the relationship and move on, making yourself available to someone who can reciprocate your love. Conversely, if you cannot love the person who's bending over backward to win your love, the kindest thing you can do is also to end the relationship and set them free to find someone who can love them in the way that you can't.

You are both free to choose to remain good friends thereafter without the expectation of a romantic relationship.

A Typical Scenario of Unrequited Love

Meet John and Jane. John has had a crush on Jane since they first met in college. Jane, on the other hand, sees John as just a friend.

Despite his feelings for Jane, John remains friends with her and tries his best to be there for her whenever she needs him. He listens to her problems, offers her advice, and even helps her move into her new apartment. However, every time John tries to take their relationship to the next level, Jane gently turns him down. She tells him that she values their friendship too much to risk it by getting into a romantic relationship. John is heartbroken, but he can't help but continue to hold onto the hope that Jane will eventually come around and see him as more than just a friend. He keeps doing everything he can to impress her and show her how much he cares, but it never seems to be enough. Meanwhile, Jane starts dating someone else, and John can't help but feel jealous and resentful. He wonders why he isn't good enough for her and why she can't see how much he loves her. As time goes on, John starts to realize that his unrequited love for Jane is holding him back from moving on and finding someone who truly loves him. He knows that he needs to let go of his feelings for Jane and focus on his own happiness. Eventually, John musters up the courage to tell Jane that he needs some space to heal and move on. It's a difficult conversation, but Jane understands and respects John's decision. In the end, John learns that unrequited love is painful but also offers a valuable lesson. He realizes that sometimes, no matter how much you love someone, it's better to let them go and find someone who loves you back.

The type of "unrequited love" I have encountered in my work is where my client is convinced they are missing the love that allows them to fully function, to finally be authentic, whole, and effective in life. They cannot do without this love but, when queried about it, they also cannot give any specifics on the who, where, how, or why of this seemingly unattainable love. You can see they are suffering as they persist in pursuing this vague, nondescript, elusive love that is supposed to be the answer to their happiness, freedom, and mobility, that allows them to finally be fully who they are.

The reason it is unrequited is that the other party has no idea my client needs their love to feel safe and supported, to prosper and flourish. And there is no way the other party can fulfill this longing and provide what is missing. So, the way it is set up is that this love lives forever as something unavailable and unattainable to my client. At the same time, it also provides a convenient excuse for them not living their full potential.

Chapter 7:

The "Glass Ceiling" of Love

The glass ceiling in the workplace is a metaphor for the invisible barrier that prevents certain people (usually women and minorities) from getting promoted and rising to senior positions in a corporation, regardless of their suitability, qualifications, and experience. It's a subtle but damaging form of discrimination, where you cannot take the opportunities you see in front of you despite your best efforts.

A curious phenomenon I have encountered time and time again in my work is what I would call a "glass ceiling" in love. It has to do with a mostly unconscious, self-imposed restriction that goes something like this: "If I go too far, become too brilliant, clever, successful, rich, independent, happy, etc., you might stop loving me." One client, Michael, goes so far as to do everything to ensure that he will not be hated, envied, or rejected. He is a kind, brilliant, lovable, and wonderful person but susceptible to control, influence, and exploitation by others.

Because belonging and connection are so important to him, he would stop himself from moving forward if he believed he would risk losing love. He would not allow himself to be rich or successful, which means he might hold back on using his skills, talents, creativity, and expertise to generate value and benefit and give his clients the "wow factor" that he is so capable of. Because he believes that being successful would mean he would have to contend with envy and hatred from others. This had been put to the test by Joseph Dominguez, author of *Your Money or Your Life*. When Joe retired from Wall Street by the age of 30, rich enough to live deliberately, meaningfully, yet frugally, he thought his father would be proud of him. Instead, his father never spoke to him again, begrudging Joe for one-upping him (Dominguez & Robin, 1992).

The "glass ceiling" in love might go something like this: I will love you as long as you promise not to do anything that will make me uncomfortable. I will love you as long as you never do anything that would challenge me, threaten me, show me up, make me feel inferior to you, or make me jealous or envious. I will love you as long as you promise not to grow, evolve, or develop. I will love you as long as you will never be more successful, happy, affluent, brilliant, and talented than I am. I will love you as long as you promise not to be who you are. I will love you as long as you promise to be who I need you to be for me to feel comfortable and secure. Otherwise, I will withhold my love and may never speak to you again.

This is a form of emotional blackmail that can come from family, friends, colleagues, and romantic partners. The thought of having love, support, and approval withdrawn stops most people cold. So, they learn that to hold onto this dubious love; they need to be someone other than themselves to be accepted or simply OK. Being authentically themselves is not safe. They must hide their brilliance, gifts, genius, talents, capabilities and even their happiness, fulfillment, and dreams just to fit in, just to be safe. They must sufficiently dumb themselves down to ensure they do not incur envy, resentment, or hatred in others. They would need to live a lie to hold on to this dubious love. That is the unspoken bargain: I will love you as long as you promise not to grow, change, evolve, develop, surpass me, threaten me, or make me uncomfortable. Whether true or not, that is the price they think they must pay to fit in, to belong, and to avoid banishment and ostracism.

Sometimes, people will tell you what they really want in life and what's really important to them. But then the years go by, and they never achieve it or even actively go after it. And they never actively go after it because of the fear of losing something very precious to them, and that very precious something is the love that never was in the first place.

In the case of two other clients, Sylvia and Beth, it's a very similar damned-if-you-do, damned-if-you-don't situation, where their fathers hate them for being successful and despise them for not being good enough. He seems to be in constant competition with her. It's as if one were playing a game where the rules make no sense and where one can never win. This often results in inaction, a kind of paralysis, and constant confusion. If she's too good, she would have to create a breakdown and a mess in order not to threaten Dad's ego or incur his wrath or envy. She is constantly adjusting, re-adjusting, and over-adjusting—too smart, too dumb, too much, too little, never just right, and all in vain. This is followed by harsh, hurtful self-criticism and self-loathing. Maybe she should be asking herself: is this really the love that supports her to come into her fullness? What would it do to her life and future relationships if she believed that this is love worth pursuing and sacrificing her life for?

Chapter 8:

Selling Out for Love

"Selling out" is a common expression for the compromising of a person's integrity, ethics, morality, values, authenticity, or principles for financial gain or mainstream power and success. It means betraying or abandoning something important for something which, under normal circumstances, your moral compass would not allow you to do. A lesser form of selling out would be where you ignore chances for personal and professional advancement to stick to a safe, comfortable job that is soul-deadening. Just as one can be corrupted by money, one can also be corrupted by love—although the latter may seem the lesser form of selling out because it can look like sacrifice, altruism, and selflessness ("selflessness" in this case would mean the abandonment of one's self).

We can sell out for money, and we can sell out for love. For instance, we may not realize until we are adults that we are living our lives to make our parents happy. This realization might come very late in life, depending on how tight a hold our family of origin has on our psyche. We may feel shocked or depressed by this information, but we can trust that it is coming to us at this time because we are ready to find out what it would mean to live our lives for ourselves by following our own calling instead of fulfilling someone else's expectations.

One of the most common reasons we are so tied into making our parents or others happy is that we were not properly nurtured and supported when we were children. We were not honored as individuals in our own right, with a will and purpose of our own. As a result, we learned to look outside of ourselves for approval, support, validation, and direction. The good news is that the part of us that was not adequately nurtured is still there, and it is never too late to provide ourselves with what we need to be who we are meant to be. If you have to give up your dreams, your aspirations, your happiness, and your soul to please someone or to hold on to their love, then the price for this kind of love is simply too high and it is no love at all. "Selling out for love" is how I would use to describe a situation where a person gives up something important to them or compromises their values, dreams, brilliance, authenticity, and personal power to please the person who, for whatever reason, is very important to them, or this might even be a group of unidentified unknown persons. I have often observed this phenomenon in my coaching clients.

This might involve betraying and abandoning their values, beliefs, and integrity to avoid rejection, jealousy, or reprisal. Often, they don't even know why they're doing it. It is driven by an irrational fear of losing the love of people who often play no part in their lives. They seem ready to throw their lives away to please a bunch of "ghosts" and give up something valuable or significant in exchange for a dubious love from a person or group of persons who often are not even aware my client needs their love. From the client's perspective, these "ghosts" are deemed responsible for providing love and, by not doing so, it's all their fault that my client is not free or empowered to live out their full potential.

One example of this condition I can give is of a brilliant professional woman, Sonja, who once easily excelled in school and who, at the age of 12, was criticized by her possibly envious girlfriends for being "too ambitious." Today she goes to great lengths to prove she is not too ambitious. To do that, she has to dumb herself down and make careless mistakes to avoid being too good at what she does. This group of girlfriends, now career women, have no clue she needs their love, approval, and permission to be who she is, but she can't give up seeking it.

She is driven to please them and win their love because only by winning their love can she finally find peace and liberation and the freedom and power to be herself. The problem is this group of women are no longer in her life and don't know this is what she desperately needs and insists on getting from them. She told me that to be without their love would be tantamount to death. Every time some breakthrough happens in our work, where she realizes she is no longer this 12-year-old girl needing the approval and acceptance of these peers, she has to create some breakdown or get sick and skip the next few scheduled sessions until this progress has a chance of becoming undone and hopefully forgotten.

Another example is of a male client who's an expert, unique, innovative, and an authority in his field but who avoids making money and being successful because he fears "being hated" by a bunch of people who play no part in his life personally or professionally. In fact, he really has to work at undermining himself and avoiding being successful and wealthy. This bunch of people he's trying to please or appease with his fake mediocrity also don't know he needs their approval, validation, and permission to be who he is. And even if they did try to give him what he needed, could he really accept this poor substitute for the once-missing parental love? He must realize that, as an adult, it is no longer appropriate to be dependent on love, support, or permission from Mommy and Daddy to survive and prosper.

Such cases are extremely tenacious, and working on them can feel like an exercise in futility. These individuals have abdicated their power to a bunch of "ghosts" in exchange for doubtful safety and love. It seems the more deprived, rejected, and frustrated they once were as a child, the more unsupported they feel and the more fixated they are to parental love. It's as if these people were under a spell that refuses to be broken. And it seems that nothing you say or do can convince them otherwise. They cannot let go because letting go would mean letting go of the chance of finally getting the parental love they so desperately yearn for.

Chapter 9:
Codependency

Codependency is a behavioral and psychological condition in which a person seeks to find their identity and happiness through another person, often at the expense of their own well-being. This can lead to a pattern of enabling behaviors and neglect of one's own needs, which can also contribute to the development of unhealthy relationship dynamics. Codependency is most often apparent in close relationships, such as romantic partnerships and family relationships.

Codependency is often characterized by poor boundaries due to a lack of separation between oneself and the other, an excessive need for approval and validation stemming from low self-esteem and self-worth, difficulty making decisions, and an inability to assert oneself. People who struggle with codependency may also tend to take care of others at their own expense, as well as to ignore or dismiss their own feelings, needs, and interests. This can lead to feelings of low self-esteem and a sense of being trapped in the relationship.

Codependency can develop as a result of growing up in a dysfunctional family environment, where there is a lack of emotional support and an over-emphasis on taking care of others. It can also be a result of past trauma or abuse.

Symptoms of codependency include:

- low self-esteem and self-worth

- reliance on others for approval, validation, and a sense of identity

- having self-limiting or self-sabotaging beliefs

- fear of abandonment

- approval-seeking or people-pleasing and being everyone's go-to person

- excessive caretaking often at the expense of one's own well-being

- dependency on others for one's happiness and fulfillment

- fear of losing control

- enduring unhealthy relationships to avoid loneliness

- giving of own finances and other resources to depletion

- having an addict, user, abuser, or narcissist in one's life

- enabling or covering up for the unhealthy behaviors of partners

You can only give so much for so long before it damages you. Being in this kind of dynamic keeps you from your authentic life path and purpose. You need to learn how to give appropriately and to set necessary boundaries without guilt or fear. You need to know when to say no to others to honor and safeguard your own sacred yes. You need to develop a stronger sense of self and to care for yourself and your needs before any healthy, interdependent relationship could be possible.

What a Codependent Relationship Might Look Like

A woman is married to a man who is an alcoholic and a narcissist. She always puts his needs before her own and thinks she can help him become sober by showing him love and affection. She is unknowingly enabling him by giving him everything he requests and covering up for his destructive behavior and irresponsibility. She blames herself for a lot of the relationship's issues and will do whatever it takes, including sacrificing her own mental well-being, to make it work. She does all this because it is preferable to being alone. Despite recognizing the toxicity of a relationship, she may struggle to leave due to feelings of guilt, obligation, fear, or a collapse of ego without the partner.

It is important to note that codependency can manifest in varying degrees and contexts, and not all of the above traits may be present in every individual. Therapy, self-awareness, differentiation, and compassion are key to overcoming this condition and building healthier relationships.

Chapter 10:
W.R.D. Fairbairn–
Theory of Object Relations

We turn to Mr. Fairbairn to help us understand how disrupted or insecure attachment bonds with caregivers can lead to certain personality disorders and difficulties in forming healthy relationships and regulating emotions in adulthood.

Fairbairn was a Scottish psychoanalyst who lived from 1889 to 1964 and is best known for his theory of object relations. The word "object" is defined as a person outside of the self, and object relations theory emphasizes the importance of early relationships in shaping personality and emotional development. Fairbairn observed that an infant is completely and utterly dependent upon their primary caregiver and is fixated on one parent as the source of all love and nurturance (Fairbairn, 1952). The quality and characteristics of this first relationship, as well as the satisfaction or frustration of the child's developmental needs, were the key factors that influenced the child's emotional development. He believed that the greatest trauma that a child could experience was not to be loved by the mother.

His most important contribution was his observation that the child's dependency on his object—whether it be a loving, nurturing mother or a neglectful and physically abusive mother—is absolute. Furthermore, the rejected child was more, rather than less, attached to the mother than the loved and accepted child was. The increase in the child's attachment was because their needs were continuously being ignored, needs that had to be met by that one and only parent. The more the child was deprived, and the more his needs were unmet, the more he was fixated. The child's attachment to the mother may destroy him, but he has no choice in the matter because his need for the mother is absolute. In 1923, Fairbairn was appointed as the Medical Officer at the Kirkcaldy Foundling Hospital in Scotland. Fairbairn became interested in the impact of early experiences on human development, and he began to study the children at the foundling homes, which provided care and safety for abandoned and abused infants and children. Fairbairn observed that many of the children showed signs of emotional and developmental difficulties, such as depression, anxiety, and an inability to form close relationships, which stemmed from early experiences of neglect and abandonment. One would expect that these abused children would be fearful and eager to escape from their parents. Instead, the children insisted that their parents were good, and they blamed themselves for the cause of all the family problems. Fairbairn was even more astonished to observe the distress and emotional collapse of these abused children after they were removed from their abusive parents and placed in the foundling home. They couldn't wait to return to their violent and dangerous parents to risk suffering more grievous injuries, and even death, rather than remaining in the sanctuary of the foundling home.

I believe the above might offer some clues as to why battered and abused women or men cannot leave a violent and dangerous environment to save their lives. Both partners come to the relationship recreating the same form of emotional attachment that they experienced as a child. With batterers, I believe the lack of emotional support during childhood does not go away but continues to build up over the years. They have an enormous reservoir of unmet needs, which are beyond anyone's ability to satisfy, and a reservoir of rage at their original parents for their deprivation of them. The batterer behaves like an empty, greedy, dependent, tyrannical infant in an adult body, demanding the maximum amount of nurturance from their symbolic mother.

They often believe that the victim is there to satisfy the deluge of unsatisfied emotional needs from childhood, to provide all the happiness they feel entitled to, and to deal with a multitude of unrealistic expectations that are practically impossible to fulfill. One of the most frequent responses to the absence of early support and nurturance in males is rage and violence directed toward others who are perceived as weaker. The rage of the neglected child has to be displaced and is most often directed at weaker others rather than at the original parents because the parents are so necessary for the survival of the child, or the now adult child. The rejected child would never confront the parent directly for being a bad parent because the child would risk retaliation, annihilation, or banishment. The victim of battering (this applies to both women and men) does not want to flee the batterer, just like Fairbairn's children who experienced extreme distress when separated from their abusive parents. Their own family of origin did not support them in developing the ego structure and identity that is essential for adulthood. Due to their developmental history, they are undifferentiated and do not have a sense of self without the abuser, whom they need to prop up their ego.

The hopeful self in the victim is attracted to the promise and fantasy of love from the partner, while the abused self is attracted to the partner's rejecting behavior. They are attracted to the same mix of antithetical emotions experienced in childhood—a pattern of alternating rejecting and loving behavior that is typical of abusers. They are unconsciously drawn to abusive partners because of personality disorders caused by childhood abuse and neglect. Sometimes when the police are called to the rescue, the victim might attack the police due to a massive dependency on her batterer. They may experience a collapse of ego if the police were to take away their desperately needed object. The victim of abuse, although terrified of further abuse, is actually less anxious when the abuser is living with them than when they are alone. This is exactly the case with Fairbairn's abused children in the foundling homes in Scotland.

We humans are generally attracted to what is familiar, even if it kills us. A lack of differentiation from the mother is key to understanding why men and women keep returning to abusive and dangerous relationships. If they are forced to function independently in adulthood, they may experience ego collapse. I have seen how the death of parents has devastated some of my clients because the death dashes all hope of ever receiving the support and nurturance that they still require and long for from the parent. The abused and neglected child needs the parent far more than the loved and emotionally supported child does.

Every child must have these four things, not just to survive, but to thrive: love, safety, significance, and connection. Certain types of early childhood deprivations guarantee that, in adulthood, the exposed child will seek out partners who recreate the original style of emotional deprivation or abuse. We need to minimize the possibility that future generations of children will be exposed to the conditions that would shape them into future abusers or victims of abuse.

The fact that their unmet childhood needs do not go away might also explain why some of my clients' attachment to the idea of mother has been replaced by attachment to a partner, a group of friends, colleagues, or even strangers—the now substitute for mother. It would seem that the bigger the load of unmet needs, the more they are hooked. Even if they realize these frustrated needs from their childhood cannot be satisfied by these substitute groups of people, they cannot let go of hoping to one day finally attain gratification of their dependency needs and get the love they think they are so desperately needing and missing.

Chapter 11:

Toxic Love

When faced with a radical crisis, when the old way of being in the world, of interacting with each other and with the realm of nature doesn't work any more, when survival is threatened by seemingly insurmountable problems, an individual life form or a species, will either die or become extinct or rise above the limitations of its condition through an evolutionary leap. –Eckhart Tolle

***

The dictionary definition of toxic: "Very harmful or unpleasant in a pervasive or insidious way" (Oxford University Press, n.d.).

A toxic relationship has unhealthy dynamics and causes you distress or harm because you're controlled, unsupported, manipulated, or disrespected. It is important to recognize signs of unhealthy relationships before they escalate. This includes:

- **Control:** One person makes all the decisions and tells the other what to do, what to wear, what to say, what to think, or who to spend time with.

- **Dependence:** One person feels that they "can't live without" the other. Or they threaten to do something drastic if the relationship ends.

- **Digital Monitoring or "Clocking":** One person uses social media sites to keep tabs on the other person and/or constantly messages or texts them demanding quick responses.

- **Dishonest:** One person lies to, steals from, or keeps information from the other.

- **Disrespect:** One person makes fun of the other in front of friends or bad-mouths them behind their back.

- **Hostility:** One person picks a fight with the other. This may lead to one person changing their behavior to avoid upsetting the other.

- **Isolation:** One person may attempt to keep the other person from friends and family.

- **Intimidation:** One person tries to control the other by making them fearful by threatening violence or a break-up.

- **Physical Violence:** One person uses force to get their way, such as hitting, slapping, punching, or kicking.

- **Sexual Violence:** One person pressures or forces the other into sexual activity against their will or without consent.

If someone is trying to control you, it can often look and feel like care. But it is actually control. And there's only one way to distinguish between care and control: is this form of care what you would want for your own well-being and for a better you, or are they doing it to make you more comfortable and convenient for them?

In a perfect world, every child would grow up in an environment of love, safety, acceptance, and belonging. This would allow them to develop appropriate and healthy levels of self-love, self-esteem, self-acceptance, self-trust, and self-respect that may safeguard them from abusive relationships and may ultimately end up protecting them and saving their lives. They would never consider abusive and controlling behavior in a relationship to be normal behavior or treatment.

Ideally, you learn about what constitutes a healthy relationship and healthy boundaries from your parents. Besides the love, care, attention, nurture, and protection from the mother, the father's role is equally important for both boys and girls. Boys need the father's physical and emotional presence, guidance, support, encouragement, and validation. He will be a role model for his son by being the type of man that he would be proud to see his daughter marry. A man might raise his daughter in this way: he makes sure she always knows that Daddy loves her, is proud of her, celebrates the fact that she is a girl, that he would always be honest with her, and that he would always have her back. All this would create a strong, confident, independent woman with a high expectation for love, respect, and honesty, and could go a long way toward keeping the wrong guy from getting a foothold.

Besides sex education, I believe that something like what constitutes a healthy romantic relationship should be taught in schools. What should you look for? What should you steer clear of? How can you tell if you are in a toxic relationship? What are the signs of an abusive relationship? How can you protect yourself? Knowledge is power. Below are some examples of personality disorders leading to unhealthy relationships with some similar qualities and overlaps, and all of them involve control.

What Is Emotional Blackmail?

Emotional blackmail is where a person who is emotionally close to you attempts to manipulate you for their own personal gain. They subtly threaten to punish you or imply that you will suffer if you don't comply with what they want. They know your deepest secrets and vulnerabilities and use this intimate knowledge to get you to comply. Whatever strengths or weaknesses you have, the blackmailer will use them against you.

Everyone knows at least one person who has used emotional blackmail tactics to force them to do something they initially refused to do. It might be a situation involving a passive-aggressive person who never seems to say exactly what they want—they just play games to get their desired result. Most people never realize the people closest to them could use this type of conscious, well-thought-out strategy; they just think of these people as being assertive or aggressive. The results of being emotionally blackmailed are always destructive.

You end up agreeing to something you never wanted to do or believed to be in your best interest. In the process of complying, the blackmailer has made you feel bad about yourself and guilty for resisting. Inevitably, you'll resent being put in that situation. A relationship that starts on such a manipulative basis is usually doomed.

Here are some of the typical threats emotional blackmailers use.

Parents and In-Laws:

- "After all I've done for you."
- "How can you be so selfish?!"
- "I'll cut you out of my will."
- "Why are you doing this? You're my own flesh and blood!"
- "I'll leave everything to charity."
- "If you don't look after me, I'll get sick and end up in hospital."
- "Don't worry about me—I'm old and will die soon."

Husbands/Wives:

- "I can't believe you're behaving so selfishly."
- "You don't really care about me."
- "If you really love me, you would…"

Ex-partners:

- "I'll drag you through the courts."
- "You'll never see the children again."
- "I'll take you for every cent you've got."

Lovers:

- "Everyone else is doing it. What's wrong with you?"
- "This is what lovers are supposed to do for each other."

- "If you really love me, you would……"

- "I would think you would have more trust in me than that!"

- "It's obvious that you don't love me."

- "It might be better if we split up."

Children:

- "All the other parents do it for their children. Obviously they love their kids more than you love me."

- "I'll run away."

- "I must be adopted."

- "You love my sister more than me."

Friends:

- "If things had been the other way around, I'd do it for you."

- "You say I'm your best friend. Well, maybe you had better find another one."

- "I've always been there for you. Look how you treat me when I need you."

Employers:

- "You'll only make things more difficult for your workmates. They'll have to carry the load."

- "I'll make sure that you're never considered for promotion ever again."

- "Surely you owe me and the company some loyalty?"

Employees:

- "If you fire me, you'll need a good lawyer."

- "I bet the media would like to hear about this."

Emotional blackmail negatively impacts a victim's self-image. If they continue to yield to the blackmailer, they will eventually lose their self-confidence and be robbed of the ability to assert themselves. They will become plagued by self-doubt, fear, and guilt, and this affords the blackmailer the power to make ever more outrageous demands.

How to Handle an Emotional Blackmailer

Emotional blackmailers usually appear to be strong and resolute. Even though they give the impression that they know what they want, and they are prepared to do what they have to do to get it, this is rarely the case. Blackmailers are usually just bullies. They have a poor self-image and can't handle rejection. They lack the maturity and self-confidence to discuss their situation and are fearful of losing what they have.

They'll usually accuse their victims of being selfish, uncaring, or self-centered when they themselves possess these traits. In many ways, they are like unruly children. They make their demand and, if it is not satisfied immediately, throw a tantrum. Every time a parent gives in to a tantrum, they are sowing the seeds of an emotional blackmailer.

Always remember, emotional blackmailers are like bullies or out-of-control children and should be treated accordingly. If you feel that you are the victim of an emotional blackmailer, you need to decide whether you are prepared to put up with it or whether you're going to do something about it.

People will treat you the way you allow them to treat you. If you are a victim, it may be because you have allowed it. The first thing to realize is that the blackmailer needs your agreement for something; otherwise, they would not be asking for you to allow them to do whatever it is they want. In reality, it's you who has the upper hand. Without your consent, the blackmailer is powerless.

The only way to lose your power is to give in to their demands. If it comes down to a compromise, set your boundaries and stay steadfastly within them. If the blackmailer is making you feel uncomfortable, refuse to go along with whatever they're proposing. Blackmailers respect people who stand their ground.

Guilt and the withdrawal of love are powerful weapons in the arsenal of the blackmailer, again, only if you allow it. When you surrender to the emotional blackmailer's initial threats, an unpleasant cycle may develop that will become progressively more difficult to stop. The blackmailer could eventually ruin the victim, emotionally and psychologically. My mother tried to saddle me with guilt when I wanted to leave home to build a life of my own. I left anyway. She seemed to have my future life mapped out for me. Emotional blackmail can trap you for life, as you stand little chance of finding happiness and love and living a life free of emotional guilt.

What Is Narcissism?

Narcissism is a personality disorder characterized by excessive self-centeredness. Many people have had exposure to a narcissist through family, work, friends, or a romantic relationship. Individuals with narcissistic tendencies have an inflated sense of their own importance, a strong need for admiration and validation, and a lack of empathy for others. They prioritize their own needs and wants over those of their partner. They may expect their partner to cater to their every whim and become angry or resentful if they don't. They often believe they are superior to others and have a sense of entitlement. They may take advantage of others for their own benefit and have difficulty forming meaningful relationships because of their lack of consideration for others' feelings and needs.

What a Relationship With a Narcissist Might Look Like

A relationship with a narcissist can be characterized by some common patterns and behaviors that can be emotionally and psychologically damaging for the other person involved. Here is a typical scenario of a relationship with a narcissist:

1. **The Love-bombing Phase:** At the beginning, the narcissist may come across as charming, charismatic, and attentive. They may shower their partner with compliments, gifts, and attention, making them feel special and loved. They may also use gifts, surprises, and grand gestures to create a sense of excitement and romance.

2. **The Idealization Phase:** The narcissist will put their partner on a pedestal and idealize them, seeing them as the perfect partner who can fulfill all their needs and desires. They may also make grand gestures, such as proposing marriage or planning an extravagant vacation.

3. **The Devaluation Phase:** As the relationship progresses, the narcissist may begin to criticize and belittle their partner. They may become emotionally distant and dismissive, and start to devalue their partner's opinions, feelings, and accomplishments. The narcissist may also become jealous and possessive, accusing their partner of being unfaithful or flirting with others.

4. **The Discard Phase:** Eventually, the narcissist may decide that their partner is no longer useful to them and discard them without warning or explanation. They may do this by ghosting their partner, abruptly ending the relationship, or cheating on them callously and without remorse. The narcissist may also blame their partner for the breakup, making them feel responsible for the failure of the relationship.

Throughout the relationship, the narcissist will prioritize their own needs and desires over their partner's, often manipulating and exploiting them to get what they want. They may be charming and seductive one moment, and cold and cruel the next, leaving their partner feeling confused, insecure, and emotionally drained. They may also engage in gaslighting, blame-shifting, and other forms of emotional abuse to control their partner and maintain their power and dominance. As a result, the other person may experience a range of negative emotions, such as anxiety, depression, trauma, and a loss of self-worth. Because of the manipulation and control tactics used by the narcissist, the partner may feel trapped in the relationship and unsure of how to leave. The narcissist may make them feel guilty or ashamed for wanting to leave, or use fear or intimidation to keep them from leaving. The relationship may be emotionally or psychologically abusive. Narcissists may use a variety of tactics to control and manipulate their partner, including gaslighting, blame-shifting, and emotional abuse. This can have a profound effect on the partner's mental health and well-being.

Overall, a relationship with a narcissist can be very challenging and unhealthy, with the partner feeling as if they were walking on eggshells and constantly trying to please the narcissist. It is self-sacrifice with no end in sight. It is important to seek help and support if you are in a relationship with a narcissist, as it can be difficult to leave on your own.

Antisocial Personality Disorder (ASPD)

I consider this a more dangerous form of narcissism. It is characterized by a pervasive pattern of disregard for and violation of the rights of others. Individuals with ASPD often engage in deceitful or manipulative behavior, with little regard for the safety, well-being, and lives of others. They are usually without principles, conscience, or remorse.

Children who experience emotional neglect, such as not receiving adequate love, attention, support, validation, or nurturance from caregivers during crucial developmental stages, may grow up with a profound sense of emptiness and inadequacy. There is an insatiable need to fill a void that simply cannot be filled by material possessions, wealth, or power. Individuals may turn to material possessions or financial success as a substitute for the emotional intimacy and connection they lacked in childhood. This can drive them to seek external validation and fulfillment through material success and accumulation of wealth. But despite their unlimited wealth, they remain poverty-stricken in heart and soul. Childhood deprivation or trauma can contribute to the development of behaviors associated with unbridled greed, where one puts profit over any regard for the pain and suffering of others. Of course, one can also be driven by past shame over financial instability and the need to compensate for this deficiency. I've often wondered how multi-billionaires never seem to experience enough. Compensation for this void can result in the prioritization of wealth and power at the expense of ethical considerations and people's lives. Everything they do has to turn a big profit, although there are services and institutions so vital to our lives that they should be exempt from privatization or market pressures. They say, "hurt people hurt people." But these people, devoid of heart, conscience, responsibility, and integrity, can kill.

It's important to recognize that childhood experiences are complex and multifaceted, and not all experiences of deprivation or trauma would necessarily lead to unbridled greed or acts of evil. Additionally, individual responses to childhood experiences can vary widely, influenced by factors such as resilience, personality, and external support systems. I think the only antidote to this condition would be massive doses of love, starting with self-love and self-respect. Just because love was missing from our past does not mean we cannot create it, generate it, spread it, and be the source of it in the present through acts of kindness, compassion, and magnanimity. It may be the only way to hammer out our own salvation and connection to life.

What Is Gaslighting?

Gaslighting is a form of psychological manipulation in which a person seeks to sow seeds of doubt in a targeted individual, making them question their own reality, memory, perception, or sanity. This is often done by denying events that have taken place, changing facts or details, and manipulating evidence to support their claims. The gaslighter would disparage your efforts and achievements, impose guilt on you, and make you take the blame so they can do whatever they want and get away with it. The goal of gaslighting is power and control—to create confusion and uncertainty, to make the target more dependent on the manipulator, and less likely to trust their own perceptions. Over time, gaslighting can lead to feelings of self-doubt, anxiety, and depression and can have long-lasting effects on a person's mental health and well-being.

Case in Point: Mary has been in a relationship with John for four months. At first, he was charming and attentive, but over time, Mary noticed that he would often contradict her and make her doubt her own memories and perceptions. For example, John tells Mary she is always trying to pick a fight when she is actually trying to be authentic, intimate, caring, and agreeable. She was looking forward to going out with him and spent time making herself look especially nice for him. He accuses her of being forgetful and chaotic and tells her that she's imagining things. He also makes subtle comments about her being overly sensitive, paranoid, and unable to take a joke. As time goes on, Mary begins to feel confused and anxious about her own reality and perceptions. She starts to question her sanity and wonders if she's losing her mind. She starts to think everything's her fault. She tries to bring up her concerns with John, but he dismisses her concerns and tells her she's being irrational. This scenario shows how gaslighting can be a subtle and insidious form of emotional abuse. It can make the victim feel helpless, confused, isolated, and at fault, and can have long-lasting effects on their mental health and well-being.

Case in Point: Linda and her husband, Sam, have been married for two years. Linda has always been confident in her memory and ability to keep track of things, but lately, she's been feeling confused and forgetful. She would swear that she told Sam something, and he would tell her she never did. Or, she would remember an event one way, and Sam would tell her it happened differently. At first, Linda thinks it's just normal forgetfulness or miscommunication. But over time, she starts to question her own sanity. She finds herself constantly apologizing to Sam for things she's sure she didn't do, just to keep the peace. One day, Linda confides in a friend about her memory troubles, and the friend suggests that Sam might be gaslighting her. Linda is skeptical at first, but as she starts to research gaslighting, she realizes that many of the tactics described sound familiar. For example, Sam will often tell Linda that she's overreacting, being too sensitive or imagining things. He'll also tell her that she's forgetful or unreliable, even when she knows she's not. He'll twist her words or deny things he's said or done, making Linda feel like she's going crazy. As Linda becomes more aware of the gaslighting, she starts to push back against it. She'll call Sam out when he's being manipulative, and she'll keep a journal to document what's happening. But Sam refuses to admit that he's doing anything wrong and accuses Linda of being paranoid. Eventually, Linda realizes that she can't change Sam's behavior and decides to leave the relationship. It takes time, therapy, and support from her friends and family, but eventually, Linda is able to rebuild her confidence and trust in her own memory and reality.

Early Signs of a Soon-to-be Abusive Partner

Early warning signs for a potentially soon-to-be abusive partner could include:

- They are love-bombing you or bombarding you with too much attention too soon.

- The relationship moves faster than you feel is normal (i.e. marriage in two weeks after meeting).

- They have rigid gender roles.

- They show signs of possessiveness and jealousy.

- They are controlling.

- They manipulate you into always doing what they want.

- They don't respect your boundaries.

- They always deflect blame.

- They isolate you from friends and family.

- They speak disrespectfully about their former partners and do not acknowledge their role in what happened.

- They have a past of domestic violence.

- You feel exhausted or drained after spending time with them.

- You feel suffocated and trapped in the relationship.

What Is Coercive Control?

Coercive control refers to a pattern of abusive behavior that's all about having power and control over another through various manipulative tactics and strategies. Unlike physical abuse, which involves acts of violence or harm, coercive control operates through psychological and emotional manipulation, aimed at dominating and subjugating the other.

Coercive control often involves a gradual and insidious process of gaining power over the victim. It is characterized by the systematic erosion of the victim's autonomy, self-esteem, and independence. The abuser uses various tactics to exert control, such as criticism, insults, threats, intimidation, humiliation, isolation, financial control, gaslighting, surveillance, and manipulation.

Intimidation plays a significant role in coercive control, as the abuser seeks to instill fear and establish dominance. This can involve verbal abuse, aggressive gestures, or a threat of physical violence, which can be more terrifying than actual physical violence. The victim may constantly fear the consequences of not obeying the abuser's demands.

Isolation is another tactic employed in coercive control. The abuser often seeks to cut off the victim from friends, family, and support networks, making them entirely dependent on the abuser for emotional and practical needs. By isolating the victim, the abuser limits their access to resources, support, and alternative perspectives, making it more difficult for the victim to leave the abusive relationship.

Financial control is a common element of coercive control, wherein the abuser controls the victim's finances, restricts their access to money, and manipulates their economic choices. This can include withholding funds, taking away their car keys, preventing the victim from working or having financial independence, and excluding the victim from all financial decisions and transactions. Gaslighting is a manipulative tactic used in coercive control to distort the victim's perception of reality. The abuser may deny or downplay abusive behaviors, invalidate the victim's emotions, and create confusion or doubt about their memory and sanity. By making the victim question their own experiences, the abuser maintains control and power over them.

Surveillance is another key aspect of coercive control, where the abuser invades the victim's privacy and monitors their activities. This can involve tracking their movements, monitoring phone calls and messages, or even using technology to maintain constant surveillance. The victim is left feeling constantly watched and controlled, which further erodes their sense of safety and freedom.

Manipulation of everyday activities is also used to enforce control in coercive relationships. The abuser may dictate what the victim can wear, where they can go, whom they can see, or even what they can say or think. By exerting control over these seemingly mundane aspects of life, the abuser ensures their dominance and establishes a power dynamic that permeates every aspect of the victim's existence.

Coercive control is a severe form of abuse that can have long-lasting psychological, emotional, and physical consequences for the victim. It often leads to PTSD. It is important to recognize the signs of coercive control and provide support and resources to those who may be experiencing it. If you are in such a relationship, tell everyone and get every resource and support to get out. By raising awareness and fostering a society that rejects all forms of abuse, we can work toward creating a safer and more compassionate environment for everyone.

In a direct communication, my friend Lynn contributed the following:

> "What if a possessive, controlling love were insidious—someone who by cruel means manipulates the object of their love to get what they want? The abuser uses their power to ignore, belittle, and cause the other person to feel doubt and insecurity, eventually resulting in the abused losing their own self-trust, with the systematic abuse continuing until they no longer react normally.

This type of relationship only exists where the abused cares deeply about the abuser who then uses this situation to their advantage. The abused blame themselves for the contempt shown towards them by the abuser, questioning whether it was something they did or said that was upsetting. They can't believe the problem is not of their making. When the toxic relationship becomes so bad that the love turns to indifference, it is particularly unhealthy. Those who are lucky enough to break free may one day find 'true love,' but not until they have come to terms with the painful memories of the past and have had a chance to restore their self-trust and self-confidence."

What is Domestic Violence

Domestic violence, also known as intimate partner violence, affects one in four women and one in seven men (Huecker et al., 2023). It refers to any form of abusive behavior that one intimate partner uses to gain power and control over the other. It can occur in any type of domestic relationship, including spouses, partners, parents, children, siblings, and other family members. There is no such thing as a typical victim. It can affect individuals of any gender, sexual orientation, race, religion, or socio-economic status.

So, keep in mind, when spotting an abuser, that they can come in any shape, size or gender, and it's not about who is more physically strong or capable; it's about control. One in three victims of abuse are men. Domestic abuse is not simply someone punching you in the face or beating you to within an inch of your life. It's much more nuanced than that. Domestic violence can have serious consequences for victims, including physical injury, mental health problems and, in severe cases, death. Domestic violence can take many forms, including:

- **Physical Abuse:** This involves any use of physical force against an intimate partner, including hitting, slapping, kicking, choking, or using weapons.

- **Sexual Abuse:** This refers to any non-consensual sexual contact, including rape, unwanted sexual advances, or forcing the victim to engage in sexual acts against their will.

- **Emotional Abuse:** This involves using words or actions to manipulate, degrade, or humiliate the victim, including verbal abuse, threats, intimidation, or isolating the victim from family and friends.

- **Financial Abuse:** This involves controlling the victim's financial resources, including withholding money, restricting access to funds, or preventing the victim from working.

- **Stalking and Harassment:** This refers to repeated unwanted contact or following the victim, both in person and online.

A Typical Scenario of Domestic Violence

Lisa and Mike have been married for 10 years and have two young children, a boy of nine and a girl of seven. Before marriage, Lisa had a job she loved as an elementary school teacher. During their courtship, Mike was Prince Charming, sweeping Lisa off her feet. She had never experienced anyone being so loving, caring, attentive, and romantic toward her. He "love-bombed" her with gifts, flowers, dinners, and constant phone calls, and proposed after only two months of dating because he loved her so much that he couldn't bear to be away from her. He convinced her to quit her job because he wanted to take care of her as an expression of his love.

Once they were married, Lisa became the wife and was expected to act like one. Mike suddenly became someone she did not recognize. He became increasingly controlling and abusive toward Lisa. It started with him criticizing her appearance and the way she dressed. If she puts on a bit of make-up and dresses in a stylish manner to please him, he tells her she's dressing like a whore to pick up men. Another thing that makes Mike angry is the sight of Lisa looking like her true self: happy, confident, and attractive. Abusers like Mike seek out beautiful and independent people like Lisa and tear them down one stitch at a time until they forget their identity—believing that the Mikes of the world are the only ones who will have them. To gain total control over her, he needs her to look awful, broken, ugly, and pathetic. He has to constantly remind her she's stupid and useless and never does anything right. He tells her she's nothing without him and nobody would want her. He controls the purse strings, who she sees, who she talks to, what she wears, where she goes, and even what and when she eats. After all, she is his property, as is everything she eats, wears, uses, and consumes. He keeps her isolated from family and friends. He regularly checks her cellphone and continuously accuses her of cheating on him when it is he who has multiple female relationships outside of marriage. Because she's such a "whore," he finally had to break her cell phone to prevent her from calling other men. She's allowed to use his phone only to call her mother, but these calls are short, strained, and supervised. Previously, Mike merely threatened physical violence but was "magnanimous" enough not to actually hit Lisa. But now it has escalated to physical violence.

Yesterday, Mike was furious at catching Lisa saying "good morning" in response to a male neighbor's greeting. He had to give her a black eye and rape her to teach her a lesson. The rapes are occurring with increasing frequency and violence. He often violates her in her sleep without her consent. Strong sleeping pills keep her from being aware of what he is doing. She has painful gynecological issues resulting from the nocturnal rapes, but he dismisses the condition as too trivial to consult a doctor about. Last night, Mike came home from work and started yelling at Lisa for not having his dinner ready. He then grabbed her by her hair and threw her across the kitchen floor. Lisa tried to defend herself, but Mike repeatedly punched her in the face and kicked her while she was down, leaving bruises on her face, arms, legs, and abdomen. Her blood was all over the kitchen floor. Mike feels that he, as the sole breadwinner, is entitled to special treatment and it is incumbent upon him to "educate" Lisa on how to be a proper wife.

What's love got to do with it? Mike tells Lisa it is she who makes him do these things, and he does these things because he loves her so much. It takes time to get a victim acclimated to the point where they feel they cannot walk away from such behavior when it does happen. A slow and steady approach is often used, so we must be aware of the earlier signs and reach out for help while we still have the strength.

The best, or rather worst, abusers are masters at assimilation, charisma, and faux-loving of their partners. They bide their time for maximum impact because they know that if they show all of themselves at once, their victim could stand up for themselves or fight back.

The story of the frog being slowly boiled to death comes to mind and is a popular metaphor for the concept of gradual change and the danger of not noticing small but significant changes over time. The story goes like this: If a frog is placed in a pot of boiling water, it will immediately jump out to save itself. However, if the frog is placed in a pot of cool water, and the heat is slowly turned up, the frog will not perceive the danger and will stay in the pot. As the water temperature rises, the frog's body adapts to the changing temperature until eventually the frog is boiled to death. This story is often used as a cautionary tale to remind us to pay attention to gradual changes in our environment so that we may act before it is too late.

Lisa is scared to call the police or leave Mike because, despite the abuse, she still loves him, is financially dependent on him, and doesn't want to disrupt her children's lives. Her children are terrorized by Mike's violent behavior. Their nine-year-old son wants to protect Lisa but only ends up getting attacked and injured as well. Lisa feels trapped and isolated, and she doesn't know what to do. She won't tell family and friends because she is so ashamed. She thinks she can and should do better and that it's all her fault that Mike is often so angry. She keeps making excuses for him, like he is stressed and exhausted from work, etc. She is hopeful that things will get better because, after the beatings, Mike's tearful apologies are so sweet and tender, bringing back those precious memories of when they first met, when he showered her with gifts and with a love she had never experienced. Little does she know, this may never happen again. Lisa is being abused and Mike will allow her very few good days for as long as he has her under his control. The "good" days, if any, will be few and far between as the bad days become the norm. If she ever does manage to leave him, he may hunt her down, stalk her, and may very well end up killing her.

Throughout the relationship, Lisa continues to defend Mike against other people's criticisms and make excuses for his violent behavior. It's as if she were afflicted with Stockholm Syndrome, a psychological condition that sometimes occurs when a hostage, or a person who has been taken captive, starts to form an emotional attachment to their captor or abuser. This attachment can manifest as feelings of trust, loyalty, and even affection toward the person who has subjected them to abuse or confinement. Stockholm Syndrome is believed to be a coping mechanism that the victim uses to deal with the trauma of their captivity. It can also be a result of a power imbalance, where the victim perceives their captor as having complete control over their life and death.

It's been said that on average, a woman will leave seven times before she leaves for good, and about 70% of these departures end in homicide ("Domestic violence statistics," n.d.). The only remedy for domestic violence is consciousness—of what it is, what it looks like, and what it feels like emotionally and psychologically. Bring it into the light—tell everyone what you're going through; seek help, support, and protection. Do everything in your power and get everything you need to protect yourself and your children to survive.

Why Me?

You may wonder what you ever did to deserve something as brutal as a toxic or dangerous relationship. These relationships are actually great teachers in disguise. This experience has nothing to do with your being at fault or making bad choices. We take different routes to get to the same destination, and the destination is to arrive at the love you need and deserve to be fully and authentically you. The road may be a hard and painful one, but we're always on the path we need to be on for our soul evolution. These relationships lead you to startling clarity about who you are and what you want. You will learn to finally set healthy boundaries, value yourself, reclaim your power, occupy your path and your life, and embody self-love and self-care. Then you will know and understand how this person has served you.

When you work through the parts of yourself that may be difficult to accept, you begin to honor yourself and move toward healing. When you walk away from a negative experience with wisdom, discernment, and clarity, the tools you gain along the way will be yours for life. You are not responsible for helping, changing, or saving another person. When it comes to soul growth and evolution, we cannot help anyone who does not want to help themselves. Like love, happiness, and gratitude, real change and growth is an inside job. Stop trying to be the savior where everyone else has failed. Change is up to the individual, and there is little you can do if they are completely resistant to shifting. When you learn to love and value yourself, you will never again let anything that even resembles a toxic relationship into your life.

We seem to be practically perfect when we live alone. It is in relationships that all that we consider flawed, ugly, and objectionable shows up. But that's why we're here. Relationships are opportunities for us to learn epic lessons and to grow, mature, evolve, and heal in a manner that serves our life's journey. We're not only here to become better; we're here to become whole—to integrate those shadow aspects of us that we would rather disown and to accept them in ourselves and in our relationships. If we never have experiences we do not want, we will never make the changes we came into this incarnation to make. Many people, after having learned their lessons and gotten complete with their past, have successfully left abusive and violent relationships to find the partner of their dreams. They felt that whatever ordeal they had to endure to get there was well worth it.

PART 3
The Love That Sets You Free

Chapter 12:
Love Is All There Is

"Love is the whole thing. We are only pieces." –Rumi

***

"Energy is all there is," is a philosophical statement that carries profound implications for our understanding of the universe and the nature of reality. Energy is everything, everywhere, all at once; it can be neither created nor destroyed. While it may seem like a simple assertion, unpacking its meaning requires delving into various scientific, metaphysical, and philosophical concepts. In the direction of the metaphysical and philosophical, it implies a holistic worldview that emphasizes the interconnectedness and unity of all things. It suggests that we are all part of a greater whole and that separateness is but an illusion. This idea challenges our conventional notions of individuality and identity, suggesting that we are not isolated entities but rather integral parts of a larger cosmic tapestry.

What if we were to regard love in the same way as we regard energy: that love is all there is, that it is the source of all existence, and that it is the only real choice we have if we want more than to merely survive? Love is like this vast ocean we are all swimming in, that we all need for our sustenance, nurture, and connection. Love is often presented as the opposite of fear, but true love is not the opposite of anything. It is the most essential and fundamental aspect of life, transcending all other emotions. It is the source that is the driving force behind human actions, relationships, and connections. It guides us in our actions and decisions and in how we interact with and treat ourselves and others.

Love connects all of us and is the ultimate source of happiness, meaning, purpose, and oneness. Love is not just something we do; it is who we are. We are the space in which love expresses and manifests itself—perhaps through our acts of magnanimity, creativity, compassion, and kindness. Love has the power to bring out what is best and most beautiful in all of us. We connect, we belong, and we complement as we pool our talents and resources to create a more beautiful, just, loving, peaceful, and harmonious world.

It is only the illusion that we are separate from this great source that causes us to believe that choosing anything other than love makes sense or is even possible or desirable. This separation can be a source of pain and suffering. The awareness that love is all there is, is who we are, and is what we are all made of, will enable us to be more peaceful, joyful, loving, and wise as we continually dwell on the question and the creation of how love expresses and manifests itself through us and our deeds.

Chapter 13:
Self-love Is the Foundation

"To love oneself is the beginning of a lifelong romance." –Oscar Wilde

***

Self-love is where it all begins. It is not selfish—you have to love and care for yourself first to be able to love and care for another. You can only love another to the extent and depth that you love yourself. Self-love is not materialistic—it's not about buying a Louis Vuitton bag or treating yourself to a spa day or a fancy dinner, although it may include these as a way of celebrating yourself and your life. Self-love is not self-care, as important as that is—taking good care of your health and well-being and developing healthy habits that support you to look your best, feel your best, and give your best.

Rather, self-love is about total self-acceptance—having compassion for yourself, coupled with gentleness, patience, humor, and curiosity while seeking to understand yourself on a deeper level, being honest with and about yourself, admitting your mistakes, and accepting and loving yourself no matter what. You take responsibility for your mistakes, but you do not wallow in self-blame, self-doubt, or self-pity. Rather than striving for perfection, you strive for growth and progress.

Self-love is the most powerful choice you can make in life. It starts with choosing to recognize that you are enough and that you are lovable, valuable, and unique, with special abilities and gifts to share with the world. There is no one else in the world exactly like you, and you have an important place and role to fill in this lifetime.

You belong, you matter, and you are meant to be here and now. The universe that created you needs you here and supports you in fulfilling your purpose. The world is a better place with you in it. You are love manifest in your loving and giving and in your contribution to life. Don't look for proof this is so. Just live it and make it your reality!

You are not your past, your childhood, your IQ, your pain, your fears, your traumas, your looks, your body shape, your weight, your grades, your bank account, your achievements, your possessions, or your successes. The ego is a never-ending race for validation, constantly seeking approval and comparing yourself to others. This is just packaging, and this is just a story. These are merely things you have; they don't define you, just as what you consider to be your flaws and failures don't define you.

Self-love requires total self-acceptance, gratitude, and embracing yourself just as you are. Self-love is authenticity and self-knowledge—you know who you are and why you're here. You do not betray your truth, integrity, principles, or values, and you can stand alone even if no one stands with you. It's the realization that there is no happily ever after. There is no finish line. There is just the journey to self-discovery, with learning and constant tweaking. Everything is a catalyst for growth. Everything in life is happening *for* you. Everything in life is rigged in your favor. It is always trial and error. It is always a work in progress.

It's not other people's job to love and respect you; it's yours. This is not something you can or should outsource. So, make sure you don't start seeing yourself through the eyes of those who don't value you. If you don't know your worth, don't expect others to. Today, let someone love you just the way you are—as flawed as you might be, as unattractive as you sometimes feel, and as incomplete as you think you are. Yes, let someone love you despite all of this, and let that someone be YOU!

You can only give and receive love to the extent that you love yourself, and the most important step to having and growing a loving relationship with yourself is to know that you are lovable, enough, significant, worthy of respect, and worthy period, no matter what. You recognize that love is and has always been all around you. You choose to be love, loving, and lovable. You choose to give and receive love freely. You choose to embrace authenticity, wisdom, healthy boundaries, and compassion. You choose to make choices that align with your truth. The magic word here is "choice" because that's where your power lies. No one can take this from you. The more love you give, the more love comes into your life—to you and through you.

You may have experienced little love in your life, but you can still choose to be filled and nourished by the abundant love that surrounds you, and you can still choose to spread this love far and wide. You can still choose to allow love to express itself through you, through your loving, caring, giving, and contribution to life. You know that you are the only person you need to love you, and you do a magnificent job of this. You are kind, generous, and forgiving toward yourself. You are your own cheerleader, best friend, ally, and doting parent. You continuously and generously shower yourself with the encouragement, praise, and acknowledgment that empower you, telling yourself what you've always wanted to hear so others can follow suit. Self-praise is about as genuine as you can get because other people's praise often comes with an agenda. They might praise you for something they want you to do or be that serves their interests rather than yours. If you fall for this or are dependent on this type of validation, you may fall under someone else's control. You stop seeking approval and validation from others because you can give this to yourself since you are your most trusted source. You constantly tell yourself what you need and want to hear while steering clear of what you don't want, what you fear, or want to avoid.

You do not have to chase love or do anything to deserve love. You don't have to be something, do something, or accomplish something to be deserving of love. No amount of wealth, success, or self-improvement is going to make up for a lack of self-love and self-acceptance. Love is an inside job. You do not have to keep searching and running after something that dwells in you, is expressed through you, and is all around you. What we long for cannot be dealt with on the outside. Nothing and no one can give you the love you need. You are free as soon as you realize that nothing and no one out there can make you happy and complete.

Self-love is a state of appreciation for yourself that grows from actions that support your physical, mental, psychological, and spiritual growth. Self-love means having a high regard for your well-being and happiness. Self-love means taking care of your own needs and not sacrificing your well-being to please others. Self-love is about taking responsibility for your creations, perceptions, and interpretations of life events. When you blame others, you remain a victim; you abdicate your power to grow, evolve, and heal. You generally attract people and experiences that match your original blueprint to allow you to take care of unfinished business. By choosing to be the master of your core issues, core beliefs, thoughts, and feelings, you choose to be the architect of your own life.

Self-love means you would never say unkind and hurtful words to yourself. It's about having a positive regard for yourself and treating yourself with the same kindness, compassion, and respect as you would your loved ones.

Ways in Which You Can Practice Self-love

There are several effective ways to harness the power of self-love, including:

- Take time to care for yourself, such as getting enough sleep, exercising regularly, and eating nutritious food.

- Say no to things that don't serve your well-being and establish boundaries with others to protect yourself from harm.

- Be kind to yourself, especially in moments of difficulty or failure, and treat yourself with the same kindness and understanding as you would a dear friend. Accept and embrace your strengths and weaknesses and prioritize your physical, emotional, and mental well-being.

- Understand your emotions, thoughts, and behaviors, and take responsibility for your actions and decisions.

- Honor, respect, and accept your feelings with no judgment.

- Recognize and celebrate your achievements, accomplishments, and unique qualities, and acknowledge your worth and value as a person.

- Choose to love yourself no matter what.

Self-love takes work and is an ongoing process. This work is your responsibility—it is your job to know, understand, accept, and love yourself first. You must first identify which relationship patterns you have learned from your parents. Then consider how these early lessons may impact your current behaviors. Then, with this insight, actively work to overcome the habits you find harmful. Understand your core issues, your unmet needs from childhood, and your vulnerabilities and traumas that impact your intimate relationships. These may include:

- fear of abandonment
- need for approval and validation
- lack of safety
- fear of rejection
- recurring distrust of others
- feeling unworthy of love
- fear of loss of control
- need for attention

To cultivate self-love, you need to embrace your complete self: your accomplishments and triumphs, together with your vulnerabilities, insecurities, and the struggles that have formed you. By moving forward with greater gentleness and understanding toward yourself, you can transform your life and enrich your relationships with grace and compassion. Self-love is about learning to identify and manage the inner fault-finding critic who has the power to create a hostile, shame-laden environment in your mind and heart. While you may never silence this voice completely, learning to recognize it and the negative impact it has on your life will help you to calm it, rather than endorsing its point of view.

A lack of self-love is often the driving force behind behaviors in our lives that cause us pain. For instance, it can manifest in destructive patterns like pursuing abusive relationships or unavailable partners, compulsive dieting, self-sabotage, addictions, and negative self-talk. When self-love isn't part of your life, you perceive yourself to be in a constant state of deficiency—as if your life would change if only you could attain the missing ingredient: "If only I got that promotion…", "If only I lost twenty pounds…", " If only I had the perfect partner..."

Usually, a lack of self-love arises from pain we've experienced in the past. And while it can be difficult, it's important to explore the origins of those hurts if we want to change how we feel about ourselves. This experience might make you feel vulnerable and raw. For instance, you might find yourself thinking about how your parents taught you to believe that love is conditional and is something you need to earn with "good" behavior. Maybe this, in turn, taught you to believe you must perform in a certain way and are not worthy of love unless you earn it.

With self-love, you become the loving and gentle friend, coach, teacher, parent, or cheerleader that's missing in your life. It will open up avenues of grace, forgiveness, support, encouragement, and peace. Fear, self-doubt, and harsh criticism will melt into nurturing compassion, appreciation, and gratitude. This is why it's worthwhile persisting through those early challenges of the journey to self-love. On the other side of struggle, deep calm, peace, and freedom await you.

A great way to be there for yourself when times are tough is to write down words of kindness and encouragement as if you were addressing a friend. Then, direct those sentiments to yourself. It might sound something like this:

> Dear Jane,
>
> You are in my thoughts and in my heart. How are you doing? I know you might be feeling low right now. And I'm here to remind you to be loving with yourself. I'm here to remind you that you're strong, authentic, beautiful, brilliant, funny, and full of light and grace. I know you will sail through this storm with serenity and aplomb like you always do.
>
> Let me take you out for dinner at your favorite restaurant or treat you to a luxurious spa day.

Be gentle and kind to yourself and know that I will always have your back and be by your side.

I am so grateful to have you in my life.

I love you.

Yours,

Jane

Keep your letter on hand—on your bedside table, in your briefcase, tucked into your wallet—so you can pull it out and read it whenever you feel your confidence and self-compassion waver.

Self-love Is About Healthy Boundaries

Do you ever stay longer at a social event than you'd like, or say yes to requests that don't suit you? Do you ever feel pressured to drink alcohol or buy things you can't afford? Do you find yourself working on your time off or missing important family functions for last-minute emergencies? Do you lack control over eating, intimacy, and alone time? If this sounds familiar, it's time to love yourself by setting healthy boundaries.

Healthy boundaries are not about controlling other people's behavior, but rather a matter of respecting your own limits and clearly communicating your needs. It starts by establishing boundaries for yourself. From there, you can build up your confidence in setting and maintaining boundaries with others.

Healthy boundaries are a way to make a relationship or experience feel honest and safe. They express what you are able and willing to accept, what you aren't willing to accept, and the consequences if other people don't respect those boundaries. Rather than keep people apart, they make trusting, authentic, and intimate relationships possible. When practicing boundary setting, don't focus on what you think you or others are doing wrong or what others must do. Instead, emphasize your feelings by using "I" statements, such as "I need" or "I feel" and how their behavior is affecting you. This prevents boundaries from turning into unilateral demands, ultimatums, emotional manipulation, playing the blame game, keeping score, or issuing punishments.

For instance, if someone is upsetting you by consistently canceling your plans at the last minute, you could set healthy boundaries by expressing how you feel. You might say:

"I feel hurt when you cancel at the last minute because it makes me think you don't value our time together."

Then, tell the other person what you need from them so that you don't feel that way:

"I need reliability to feel like you care about me. Can you please put our dates in your calendar so you can remember ahead of time that we're meeting?"

By focusing on your emotional experience instead of the other person's behavior, you open up the space for collaborative discussion and resolution.

Your Feelings Matter

Hurt, rage, grief, shame, fear, terror, loneliness, despair, and so on—all of these tend to get lumped together as "negativity." There are feelings we don't want to feel or admit to, so we judge them and suppress them. Trying to escape or numb ourselves from our pain or negative feelings only serves to keep them in place—in our body or psyche and beyond our control—leading to emotional disconnection or dissociation. Keep something in the dark long enough and it will probably behave badly. However, if that negative feeling were fully experienced, fully felt, and skillfully approached, it would free us to live more deeply and more fully. Feelings are merely messengers—they are there to tell us something or teach us something. And they are relentless when it comes to delivering our message to us. They will not go away until we open the door, accept the delivery, and sign for it. The real concern isn't whether to express our "negative" feelings but how we choose to express them. Beyond the polarity of holding them in and directly expressing them, we need to infuse them with love, compassion, acceptance, ease, recognition, presence, and vitality. We need to humanize, occupy, and embrace them fully. Peace, freedom, and aliveness are the rewards.

Vulnerability Can Be Our Superpower

In self-love, vulnerability can be the key to deeper, more fulfilling relationships. If we can be vulnerable with ourselves, we can be vulnerable with others and allow them to be vulnerable as well. Our feelings matter; they are an important part of us that deserves to be fully and lovingly acknowledged. Vulnerability is often seen as a weakness because it involves opening ourselves up to the possibility of being hurt or rejected. However, vulnerability can also be a strength because it allows us to connect with others on a deeper level and forge stronger relationships. We often find that once we have revealed some sensitive part of ourselves, it may also cease to be so sensitive.

When we allow ourselves to be vulnerable, we allow ourselves to be authentic, which can help others to trust and relate to us more easily as we bring out the same in them. It also allows us to learn and grow from our experiences, as we are more open to feedback and new perspectives. Being vulnerable can also lead to increased empathy and compassion for others, as we become more attuned to the struggles and challenges that they may be facing.

Vulnerability is a strength because it allows us to be more fully human, with all our flaws, insecurities, and imperfections, and to embrace all that we have and all that we are with no apology. It is the true test of self-acceptance. Our vulnerability ultimately makes us powerful and whole. It takes courage to be vulnerable, and the rewards are profound. It is not easy to expose our true selves, as it involves the risk of rejection or judgment. It is crucial to remember that vulnerability is not about seeking validation from others but about embracing our authenticity. We must be gentle and compassionate with ourselves as we navigate the vulnerability journey.

By embracing vulnerability, we invite others to do the same. We create an environment of trust and openness, fostering deeper connections with the people around us. Through vulnerability, we encourage empathy and compassion, as others can relate to our struggles and find solace in knowing they are not alone.

Vulnerability can be the gateway to personal growth, personal development, and healing. We allow ourselves to feel what needs to be felt. We acknowledge our vulnerabilities to confront them and work toward self-improvement. By recognizing our limitations and embracing our weaknesses, it is in these moments of vulnerability that we can uncover our true potential and find the strength to overcome challenges.

In relationships, vulnerability is essential for intimacy and closeness. Opening ourselves up to another person creates a space for deep emotional connection and moves us beyond the shallows of relationships. Daring to share our fears, dreams, and desires with someone builds a foundation of trust and understanding. It is through vulnerability that we can finally be and feel seen, heard, and accepted for who we truly are.

In conclusion, vulnerability is a powerful force that can transform our lives. It is through vulnerability that we find the courage to show our true selves, invite others to do the same, and foster authentic relationships. Vulnerability allows us to confront our limitations and embrace wholeness. It opens us up to the richness of life and enables us to savor its joys and challenges. Embracing vulnerability is an act of self-love, self-acceptance, and courage, and it has the potential to shape our lives in extraordinary ways.

Chapter 14:

Unconditional Love

You don't love someone for their looks or their clothes or their fancy car but because they sing a song only you can hear. —Oscar Wilde

I find the best way to love someone is not to change them but instead help them reveal the greatest version of themselves. —Steve Maraboli

***

Unconditional love is showing love for another person without considering how it will benefit you or what you will get in return. In the purest sense, unconditional love is about caring about the happiness and well-being of another person without any concern for how it benefits you. Unconditional love is a selfless act. It is love with no strings attached. You're not in it for yourself. It's love you offer freely. There is no "because" behind "I love you." There is no quid pro quo. You don't base it on what you get out of it or on what someone does for you in return. You simply love them because you love them, and you want nothing more than their happiness and well-being. Unconditional love is altruistic. Altruism refers to helpful actions taken to support and benefit others, sometimes at your own expense. It means you don't consider any potential benefits of loving someone. You offer your love for their support and benefit. It is debt-free. It is not a give-to-get. It is not given to get something, to look good, for self-enhancement, or self-aggrandizement.

Agape

This type of love, sometimes called agape, might bring to mind the love parents might have for their own children. Agape is a Greek term that refers to a kind of love that is unconditional and selfless. Agape is not based on the recipient's qualities, actions, or merits, but rather is freely given and undeserved. It is often described as a spiritual or divine love and is characterized by its generosity, compassion, and benevolence. Agape is often regarded as the highest and purest form of love. It might be reflected in one's general love for humanity. In practice, agape can manifest in various ways, such as forgiveness, compassion, altruism, and service to others. In agape, you are the source of love.

The more agape you express and extend, the more abundant and enriched you become. Everyone wants to be loved for who they are and without conditions. Having someone love you for yourself, just as you are—no matter what—is the most empowering, liberating, and healing love you can experience. This type of love is what I believe I experienced in the first years of my life in my community in China. It is not something most people encounter in life, but it is definitely worth holding out for. Besides, why should we settle for anything less?

Unconditional Love's Impact on Emotional Health

Receiving unconditional love can make a huge difference in one's emotional well-being. One has a better chance of growing up more loving, caring, giving, and compassionate toward oneself and others. Children who receive high levels of affection from their parents or caregivers tend to have greater resilience in adulthood and experience fewer mental health symptoms. Loving children unconditionally improves their lifelong health and wellness. This suggests parental unconditional love could offer some protection against the harmful and pervasive effects of childhood trauma and abuse.

When You Were Born

To set them up for life, all children need these four things to survive and thrive: love, safety, significance, and connection. How do you think your child would turn out if they started their life like this? When you were born, ideally you should have been welcomed with anticipation, excitement, and gratitude in the loving arms of both of your happy, beaming parents. They could hardly wait to welcome you into the world and into their lives. The message you got from them should have sounded something like this: "Welcome, you little bundle of joy! We are so excited you are finally here! We're so grateful and proud to be your parents. We love you completely and unconditionally. We love you exactly the way you are. The world is so much better with you in it.

There is nothing you can't do. There is nothing you have to do or to be for us to love you. You are beautiful. You are precious. You are perfect. You matter. You are significant. We will always be there for you. We will always have time for you. We will always listen to you. We are going to have a wonderful time together!"

You Feel Secure

Unconditional love can provide a sense of safety and security in both childhood and adulthood. Feeling confident in someone's love and acceptance and knowing it won't go away can help create and foster autonomy, independence, and self-worth. If you know your parents or caregivers will continue to love you even after you make mistakes or do things they don't approve of, you'll feel more comfortable making your own choices and learning from them as you go.

In the context of friendship, unconditional love might weather tests like conflict, competition, distance, or differing life interests or goals.

When it comes to romantic relationships, unconditional love could mean that love doesn't go away, despite challenges like life-altering health conditions or changes in appearance or personality or fortune.

It Involves Acceptance and Forgiveness

People aren't perfect, and anyone can make choices they regret. Unconditional love, however, requires unconditional acceptance. So, you forgive mistakes and continue to offer love and acceptance, even if their choices distress or hurt you. Your unconditional love remains unchanged despite their actions. You can, however, love someone unconditionally without having a relationship with them. Acceptance sometimes involves recognizing that it's unlikely someone will change and taking steps to protect your own well-being. Unconditional love is not without healthy boundaries, self-love, and self-respect.

What It Isn't

Although unconditional love is about the total acceptance of someone, it does not mean tolerating abuse, neglect, or other deal-breakers. Unconditional love should not be painful or harmful.

Confusion and misconceptions about the true nature of unconditional love can seem to suggest this type of love tolerates unhealthy or toxic relationship dynamics. There's an important distinction between offering love and forgiveness versus continuing to accept abusive and harmful actions and behaviors.

You Do Not Ignore Relationship Issues

Conflict is normal (and healthy) in relationships. Unconditional love doesn't mean you let someone walk all over you, you avoid conflict, or ignore problematic behavior. If they do something to violate your trust, disrespect you, or disregard your needs and wishes, you might not stop loving them, but neither do you ignore the breach of trust. Depending on the circumstances, you might agree to work together to resolve the issue and rebuild trust, but you might also see no future in the relationship. You might walk away while still holding forgiveness and love in your heart.

You Do Not Neglect Your Own Needs

Attempting to meet all your partner's needs can seem like one way of expressing unconditional love, but this can actually create an unhealthy dynamic in your relationship. No one person can nor should provide another person with everything they need. You should feel free to set boundaries around things you don't want. Unconditional love is not selfless; it doesn't mean you give up who you are and what's important to you. It's essential to take care of your own needs and wants, or you won't be in any position to love and support someone else.

Safety Is a Must

Safety is a basic human need. Unconditional love doesn't mean staying in an unhealthy or unsafe situation when you're better off letting it go. You can express forgiveness and love even after safely leaving the relationship. Blanket tolerance for harmful behavior can prevent them from making needed changes. The responsibility for their actions rests entirely in their hands, not yours.

When Conditions Change

Consider the love you have for your partner or anyone else. What triggered it originally? Perhaps you felt attracted to certain specific characteristics: a sense of humor, a kind heart, or intelligence. What if they no longer possess those characteristics? Would your love continue as always? If conditions never change, you might never know whether your love truly is unconditional.

In reality, love can grow, shift, change, and fade over time. Love changes, in part, because people change. You, or your partner, may not be the same person years down the line. Instead of seeking out an idealized, potentially unattainable type of love, try for a more realistic goal: mature, nurturing love founded on wisdom, compassion, and respect.

Also, what about those people in your tribe or clan? Do you love them mainly because they are like you—the same race, religion, education, class, social and economic background as you? Or, can you extend the same humanity, compassion, acceptance, and respect to people who are different from you?

Unconditional Love in Romantic Relationships

Romantic love is, to many people, the pinnacle of life experiences. Falling in love with someone can feel exciting, even exhilarating. But over time, these feelings may settle into something that feels a little different. You might find yourself going from, "I'm in love with them," to, "I love them." Loving someone, instead of feeling "in love" with them, simply illustrates how feelings of love evolve over the course of a relationship, especially a long-term relationship.

For love to thrive, there must be healthy boundaries. Unconditional love in romantic relationships doesn't entail a loss of self; it doesn't mean always giving people what they want or accepting what they do at the expense of your own needs and safety. You honor their requests when you can do so without sacrificing or harming yourself. You are assertive by letting them know where you stand so that you can work out the best outcome for the two of you together. If your partner doesn't respect your boundaries, your space, and your privacy, the relationship isn't going to work, no matter how deeply you love them. Moving on from it, then, could be considered an act of unconditional self-love.

To feel safe in a relationship, both parties need to feel respected and supported, to know that the other has your back, and that they are committed to loving you unconditionally no matter what the future brings. You need the safety and freedom to be authentically you without fearing rejection, abandonment, or the loss of love. People are usually programmed for conditional love. You love your partner because of their unique traits and qualities that attracted you to them.

It's why you love them in the first place. The question becomes what if they change? At what point is love withdrawn? After the exhilaration dies, the beauty fades, and the wealth dissipates, what remains? This is the point where love becomes a choice borne of freedom, rather than a feeling. That is the true test of unconditional love, or whether there was love at all. It is a mature type of love that treats the other with love and respect while maintaining your boundaries and standing up for yourself. Whereas the immature version of unconditional love would have you feeling as though you must be everything to the other person, the mature version has you recognize that your only obligation is to be true to yourself and to honestly communicate your needs and wants while honoring theirs. Neither party is more important than the relationship.

For love to thrive, both parties must go into it 100%, each willing to do the necessary hard work that eventually pays off in greater trust, confidence, closeness, intimacy, freedom, and fulfillment. This also includes, but is not limited to, the following:

You Respect Even When You Disagree

You and your partner are two different people, so it makes sense you'll have differences of opinion from time to time. Conflict and disagreement aren't necessarily problematic. It can even improve the quality and health of your relationship when handled productively and constructively. When navigating conflict, it's important to accept any differences with respect. You can disagree without being disagreeable.

You want to send a message that says, "I disagree with you, but I do love you and respect your point of view." Once you have both expressed your views, you can begin working toward a resolution.

You Practice Open Communication

Good communication should be clear, honest, and timely. You show your respect and commitment to working through challenges and finding ways to meet conflicting views by bringing up issues as they arise. You get in touch with your feelings, and you share them openly and honestly, but you also listen attentively to what your partner has to say. You make sure to get clear on what you don't understand to better prevent conflict in the future. Most of us are not used to communicating in this way. But the rewards are greater trust, openness, safety, and intimacy.

You Support Each Other

Most relationships that thrive involve plenty of mutual respect and support. When your partner struggles, you listen with empathy or offer a helping hand, and they do the same for you. You stay mindful of their needs as well as your own, and they know you have their back when they're up against something they can't handle alone. A time may come when you find yourself sacrificing something for their benefit. In a healthy relationship, sacrifice should go both ways. It involves both give and take so that both parties can experience being supportive and supported as needed.

Chapter 15:
Differentiation of Self

Be who you are and say what you feel, because those who mind don't matter, and those who matter don't mind. –Bernard M. Baruch

You were not meant to blend in; you were meant to stand out. –RuPaul

***

Differentiation of self is a psychological state in which one can maintain one's sense of self, identity, thoughts, and emotions within close and intimate relationships. It involves being able to think for oneself, make decisions independently, and assert one's own needs and values while remaining emotionally connected to others. One can separate personal feelings and thoughts from those of family, partners, and friends, enabling one to maintain a healthy balance between emotional connection and autonomy in relationships. Highly differentiated individuals learn these skills from caregivers with high levels of differentiation. It is a crucial and lifelong process for the development of healthy individuals and healthy relationships.

Differentiated individuals possess healthy and appropriate boundaries. They can maintain their beliefs and attitudes and not give in to the pressure to conform to external expectations. They have a clear sense of direction and purpose for their lives. They do not change or tailor themselves to suit others or to avoid conflict. They do not become engulfed or enmeshed in the thoughts and emotions of others. They are honest and assertive and do not give in for the sake of keeping the peace, and they expect their partners to behave similarly. In the face of conflict or disagreement, they are open and receptive to the perspectives of others. Another hallmark of differentiation is self-validation. They do not rely on external validation for internal self-worth and do not allow others' criticism, opinion, or judgment to unduly influence them, especially if it does not serve their best interests. They focus on achieving their own goals and honoring their own values. Furthermore, differentiated individuals can self-soothe without the aid of substances, reliance on their partners, or unhealthy coping mechanisms. They possess an ability to manage and tolerate difficult feelings. They are more resilient and flexible in the face of difficulties and challenges. They can bounce back from setbacks to pursue their goals without being overwhelmed by adversity.

Self-differentiation and self-love are intertwined processes that involve setting and maintaining healthy boundaries while in relationships with others. Self-differentiation encourages authenticity and self-acceptance, allowing individuals to embrace their strengths, weaknesses, and unique qualities. Self-love flourishes when individuals can fully accept themselves, flaws and all, without seeking validation or approval from others. Self-differentiation involves developing a strong sense of autonomy and independence. When individuals can stand firm in their beliefs, values, and needs without feeling overly influenced by others, they are more likely to cultivate a deep sense of self-worth, self-trust, and self-respect, which are essential components of self-love.

Chapter 16:
Love in a Mature Relationship

Love has nothing to do with what you are expecting to get, only with what you are expecting to give—which is everything. –Katherine Hepburn

Love is that condition in which the happiness of another person is essential to your own. –Robert A. Heinlein

***

Love is the most beautiful, powerful, and transformative emotion that exists. It has the power to bind souls together, to ignite the flames of passion, and to transcend the boundaries of time and space.

Imagine a love so profound, so limitless, so pure, that it becomes a force capable of setting one free. It is a love that empowers and liberates the spirit. It is a love that embraces both individuality and togetherness, creating an exquisite balance between freedom and connection. In this love, there is an unspoken understanding that each person's growth and happiness are intertwined. It encourages and supports the blossoming of dreams and the pursuit of personal passions.

At its core, a love that sets you free is built on trust. It is a sanctuary where vulnerabilities can be shared without fear of judgment or rejection. It thrives on open communication, openness, and trust, allowing both partners to express their deepest desires and concerns, and to work together toward a shared vision of happiness. In this love, there is a profound acceptance of each other's flaws and imperfections, fostering an environment where personal growth can flourish.

This love encourages independence and self-discovery. It recognizes that true freedom lies not in detachment, but in the ability to nurture one's own passions and aspirations while remaining deeply connected to another soul. It is a love that celebrates individuality, supporting the exploration of personal dreams and encouraging the pursuit of personal goals. In a love that sets you free, there is an unwavering sense of support and encouragement. It is a love that empowers, lifts, and inspires. It provides a safe haven where risks can be taken, where failures are seen as opportunities for growth, and where successes are celebrated with joy and pride. In this love, there is no room for jealousy or possessiveness. Instead, there is a deep-rooted belief in the limitless potential of each partner and a commitment to fostering that potential.

This love is not without its challenges, for no journey towards freedom is ever without obstacles. But in the face of adversity, this love stands strong, resilient, and unyielding. It is a love that weathers storms and navigates rough waters. This love understands the value of compromise and the power of forgiveness. It is a love that, even in moments of disagreement or conflict, finds a way to foster growth, compassion, and understanding.

A love that sets you free is a transformative force that liberates the soul from the shackles of fear, insecurity, and self-doubt. It encourages the pursuit of authenticity and truth, and it offers solace and warmth amid life's uncertainties. It is a love that encourages exploration, playfulness, adventure, and self-discovery. It respects and supports each other's boundaries, privacy, and mysteries. It is a love that, ultimately, propels both individuals toward their highest potential, while remaining deeply interconnected and interdependent. It creates an environment where both partners can soar to unimaginable heights.

A love that sets you free transcends the conventional boundaries of relationships and empowers individuals to grow, explore, evolve, and discover their true selves. It is a love that nurtures personal freedom, encouraging both partners to pursue their dreams, aspirations, and individual paths. This kind of love is built on trust, understanding, and a deep respect for each other's autonomy.

There is an inherent belief in the limitless potential of each person. Partners understand that personal growth and self-fulfillment are essential for a flourishing relationship. They support and encourage each other's endeavors, providing a safe and non-judgmental space for exploration. There is an understanding that individuals are responsible for their passions, purpose, and happiness, and this love empowers and supports them to do so. Communication plays a vital role in a love that sets you free. Partners openly express their desires, dreams, and fears, creating a strong foundation of trust and understanding. They dare to be vulnerable because they feel safe. They listen to each other with empathy and seek to comprehend their partner's perspective. This open dialogue allows for the expression of individual needs and helps avoid feelings of suffocation or restriction within the relationship.

In a love that sets you free, there is a profound sense of support and encouragement. Partners celebrate each other's successes and provide a shoulder to lean on during challenging times. They acknowledge that personal growth may involve taking risks, stepping out of comfort zones, and embracing change. Through their steadfast support, they help each other overcome obstacles, develop resilience, and blossom into their best selves.

Jealousy, possessiveness, domination, and engulfment have no place in this kind of love. Instead, there is a deep sense of security and confidence in the relationship. Partners trust each other implicitly, recognizing that their love is not dependent on controlling or owning one another. They understand that true love is about nurturing the happiness, growth, and well-being of each other, even if it means granting them the freedom to explore other interests or relationships without breaching each other's trust in the process.

A love that sets you free prioritizes self-love and individual well-being, reminding each partner to take care of themselves physically, emotionally, mentally, and spiritually. Partners understand the importance of personal space and alone time. They recognize that solitude, privacy, and self-reflection are crucial for maintaining a healthy sense of self.

Commitment becomes an open-eyed, resolutely empowered yes to a well-considered choice. The commitment is rooted in a deep emotional bond and a shared vision for the future. Partners happily and freely choose to be together, not out of obligation or fear of loneliness, but because they genuinely cherish each other's presence and believe in their shared journey. This love is built on mutual respect, admiration, and a profound connection that transcends any restrictions or limitations.

True love is a complex and multi-faceted concept that generally involves a deep and authentic emotional connection between two people that is based on a mutual vision, respect, support, trust, and affection. You love the other for no reason—for no if, when, or because. You love them exactly the way they are right now, not for who you hope they might become in the future. It involves a strong sense of commitment and devotion to the other person and a willingness to make sacrifices for their happiness and well-being.

True love is not just about feeling intensely positive emotions; it is not just about sex, attraction, safety, security, and validation. It involves maturity, wisdom, compassion, and the ability to navigate through difficult times and challenges together and work through conflicts constructively and compassionately. True love is characterized by a joint vision of the relationship and a deep commitment to the relationship. It is characterized by a sense of understanding and empathy for the other person, and a desire to support and uplift them in all aspects of their life. It is a selfless and unconditional form of love that transcends physical attraction or superficial qualities.

True love only delivers what we put into it. We need to ask not only what we want from such a relationship but also what we are willing to do to manifest that. Yes, you can have it all. If you are willing to put in the work, you will eventually reap the rewards—to be healed, awakened, transformed, and deepened through your relationship. It won't necessarily be an easy ride, but the very difficulties and challenges that we face provide most of the raw material for reaching the depth, joy, fulfillment, and ease of relationship for which we yearn.

In conclusion, a love that sets you free is a transformative and liberating experience that empowers individuals to be their authentic selves, pursue their passions, and grow individually while maintaining a deep connection to each other. It is a love that promotes trust, open communication, and steadfast support. It encourages personal freedom, self-fulfillment, and the celebration of each other's individuality and differences. It is a love that allows both partners to soar to new heights while knowing they have a loving and secure base to return to. In a love that sets you free is the knowledge that every relationship you have is mirroring something about you that wants to come into consciousness for your wholeness, healing, transformation, and the evolution of your soul. Some aspect of you is being mirrored that you may not want to see or acknowledge, but that presents an opportunity for growth and transformation. Whatever is going on between the two of you is happening for a powerful purpose. You can love someone and deeply care for them without taking responsibility for their feelings, actions, behavior, beliefs, or thoughts. It is the freedom to be fully who you are while allowing them to be fully who they are without trying to change, manipulate, fix, or control them. Each can simply be who they are while loving the other just as they are, letting go of wanting or needing them to do or be any other way. Instead of being engulfed, enmeshed, or losing yourself in love, instead of devolving into half of a couple, you rise in love, you evolve, expand, and transform in love, while allowing and supporting each other to become all that you are meant to be.

Chapter 17:

Compassion

A human being is a part of the whole called by us Universe, a part limited in time and space. He experiences himself, his thoughts and feelings, as something separated from the rest, a kind of optical delusion of his consciousness. This delusion is a kind of prison for us, restricting us to our personal desires and to affection for a few persons nearest to us. Our task must be to free ourselves from this prison by widening our circle of compassion to embrace all living creatures and the whole of nature in its beauty. —Albert Einstein

There is no exercise better for the heart than reaching down and lifting people up. — John Holmes

***

Compassion is an emotional response that is characterized by a deep sense of empathy, concern, and understanding for the suffering or misfortune of others. It involves the ability to put oneself in someone else's shoes and truly understand their pain, struggles, and challenges.

When we experience compassion, we feel a genuine desire to help, comfort, or uplift those who are going through difficult times. It puts us in touch with our capacity for empathy, which allows us to recognize and resonate with the feelings and experiences of others. It takes us from "we versus they" to "we and they" and finally to "we are they."

While it is easy to extend kindness and generosity to family, friends, and people who are like us in every way, the test of true compassion is when we can treat those who are very different and far less fortunate than we are with dignity, respect, sensitivity, consideration, and benevolence. Rooted in the recognition of our shared humanity, compassion transcends differences and fosters a sense of connection and solidarity among individuals and communities. Compassion goes beyond mere sympathy or pity. It is an active force that propels individuals to take meaningful action to alleviate suffering and promote well-being. Whether it is providing a listening ear, offering practical assistance, or advocating for social change, compassion manifests in various forms. It prompts acts of kindness, generosity, and selflessness as individuals extend themselves to make a positive difference in the lives of others.

One of the remarkable aspects of compassion is its ability to transcend boundaries and differences. It does not discriminate based on factors such as race, religion, nationality, or socioeconomic status. Compassion bridges divides and nurtures a sense of shared humanity, fostering understanding, tolerance, and acceptance among people. It cultivates a sense of unity that acknowledges the interconnectedness of all beings.

Moreover, compassion is not limited to helping others on an individual level; it also extends to addressing systemic issues and promoting social justice. Compassionate action involves identifying and challenging the root causes of suffering and working towards creating a more equitable and just society. It involves standing up against discrimination, oppression, and inequality and advocating for policies and practices that promote fairness, inclusivity, and equal opportunities for all.

Self-compassion

Cultivating compassion within ourselves and our communities is essential for creating a more compassionate world. It starts with nurturing self-compassion, which involves extending kindness and understanding to ourselves, recognizing our own pain and struggles, and treating ourselves with love, care, and forgiveness. By cultivating self-compassion, we develop the capacity to extend compassion to others more readily and authentically.

Self-compassion requires that we stop being negative about our negativity or our unwanted feelings, as this splits us off from our unresolved wounds. Hurt, rage, grief, shame, fear, terror, loneliness, despair, grief, and so on—all of these tend to get lumped together as "negativity," as something far from spiritual. But all we've really done is escape from the very pain that, if fully felt and skillfully approached, would free us to live more deeply, more fully, and more authentically. Our lack of intimacy with our unwanted feelings and other painful states keeps our experience superficial, emotionally anemic, and addicted to whatever helps numb us to our negativity. The real concern isn't whether or not to express our "negative" feelings, but how to express them constructively and responsibly. For instance, beyond the polarity of suppressing our anger and directly expressing our anger is the possibility of a truly healthy capacity for both the containment and release of anger that is infused with compassion, clarity, and vitality.

Instead of trying to transcend your negativity, get intimate with it. Reclaim it and embrace it fully so that it becomes a vital part of your power and energy. Stop relegating it to the shadows. Express these feelings with responsibility, intention, and compassion until they are no longer negative, until they no longer need to be felt, and until all that remains is love, ease, recognition, presence, aliveness, wholeness, and connectedness.

Compassion is a quality that can be cultivated through intentional practices such as mindfulness, active listening, and engaging in acts of kindness. Such acts of kindness can be nurturing, uplifting, and healing and might save someone's life. By cultivating awareness and presence, we become more attuned to the suffering of others and develop a greater capacity for empathy, understanding, and right action. We can actively seek opportunities to connect with others, listen deeply to their stories, and offer support and assistance as needed.

Compassion, at its core, is the embodiment of love. It is a deep and profound understanding of the suffering of others, accompanied by a genuine desire to alleviate their pain. When we engage in acts of compassion, we tap into the essence of what it means to be human—to connect, empathize, and extend kindness where needed.

Love, often seen as an emotion, is more than just a fleeting feeling. It is a force that transcends boundaries and unifies us as a species. Love encompasses empathy, understanding, and the recognition that we are all interconnected. Compassion, therefore, is a manifestation of this love—a practical expression of our shared humanity. Compassion recognizes that we have the power to make a positive difference in the lives of others. It is through acts of compassion that love becomes tangible, transforming lives and creating a ripple effect that spreads throughout society, while we, in turn, are enriched and transformed as a result. In a world often characterized by division and strife, compassion is the unifying force. It bridges the gaps that separate us—whether they be cultural, social, or ideological—and reminds us of our shared vulnerabilities and aspirations. Compassion dissolves the illusion of separation and reveals the interconnectedness of all beings. It reminds us that we are part of a larger whole, that we are in this together, and that our actions have the potential to impact the lives of others in profound life-giving ways.

Moreover, compassion is not limited to our interactions with fellow humans. It extends to all living beings, recognizing their inherent worth and the interconnectedness of all life forms. It urges us to extend our love and care to the animal kingdom and the environment, acknowledging the delicate balance that sustains our planet. We would not encroach on the natural habitats of beautiful creatures. We can start being responsible toward nature in small steps, like reducing plastic and waste and using resources consciously and only as needed. As a result, existence may start restoring and replenishing itself because that is its nature.

Compassion is a transformative force. It has the power to heal wounds, mend broken relationships, and bring about positive change. When we approach others with compassion, we create an environment of trust, acceptance, and understanding. It allows for forgiveness and reconciliation, fostering a sense of unity, peace, and collective growth.

By cultivating compassion within ourselves and our communities, we contribute toward creating a more caring and empathetic world. In cultivating compassion, we cultivate love. Compassion is the embodiment of love. We become love personified, spreading kindness and understanding wherever we go. Compassion empowers us to make a difference, however small it may seem, with one act of kindness at a time. Let us embrace compassion as a guiding principle and unleash the transformative power of love in our lives and in the lives of others. Love is not just something we do; it's who we are. We are instruments of love, which is the music coming through us. And the more we practice, the more mellifluous the sound!

Chapter 18:
Forgiveness

To err is human; to forgive, divine. –Alexander Pope

Forgiveness is the fragrance that the violet sheds on the heel that has crushed it. –Mark Twain

***

Why Forgive?

You forgive because, above all, you want peace, freedom, and healing for yourself. And, for that, you would be willing to let go of any anger, resentment, bitterness, and retaliation that could ultimately destroy you. You simply write off the "debt." You let go of needing to be right. You show compassion first to yourself as an acknowledgment that you, too, are a fallible, imperfect human being capable of making mistakes and then extending this compassion and humanity to the offender.

Before you forgive, you need to identify the wrongdoing and non-aggressively communicate it to the wrongdoer so that they become aware of what they have done. Then, you separate the act from the person. This allows you to connect with their humanity as you would your own. Forgiveness doesn't mean excusing someone's behavior. In fact, without the recognition of a wrong, there can be no forgiveness.

Forgiveness does not mean you condone the transgression or a lack of accountability or forgoing justice. People who commit crimes must understand the consequences of their actions and make amends. Next, you absorb or write off the debt you think is owed you. When you do this, you release the wrongdoer from their liability, and you release yourself from the need to be right (and miserable). You free yourself from being emotionally tied to the offender any longer than necessary.

You reclaim your power and energy. Holding on to anger, resentment, and thoughts of retaliation is like drinking poison and hoping the other person dies. Finally, the goal of forgiveness is to restore fellowship. You support the wrongdoer's efforts to correct their mistake, to change, and to make amends. You have the responsibility to approach the person to let them know they have wronged you and, if they make amends and do everything in their power to make it right with you, to pursue reconciliation and fellowship with them.

When we ask for forgiveness, we should be willing to admit our transgressions and do the work that's needed to make things right. Wrongdoing creates a rift between the offender and the offended that requires healing, which is important to stop the subconscious transmission of hurt to other people.

Forgiveness has a number of psychological, emotional, and even physical benefits. Forgiveness has been shown to reduce anxiety, depression, and stress, and to increase feelings of hope, gratitude, peace, and self-esteem. Forgiveness can help to repair damaged relationships and improve communication. It can also prevent conflicts from escalating and damaging the relationship further. It can free up the emotional energy that's tied to the wrongdoer. It has been linked to lower blood pressure, decreased stress hormone levels, and a stronger immune system, all of which can contribute to better physical and emotional health. Forgiveness can also be a spiritual practice, helping us to develop a more compassionate and loving attitude towards others, as well as ourselves, since we are all fallible human beings.

It is worth noting that forgiveness is a personal process with many benefits for the forgiver. While forgiveness doesn't mean forgetting or excusing harmful behavior, letting go of anger and resentment to get to a place of peace, freedom, and healing is imperative to our physical, mental, emotional, and spiritual well-being. Forgiveness is not about taking a moral high ground. We do it first for ourselves. When we practice forgiveness, we replace feelings of rancor and self-righteousness with peace of mind, greater emotional well-being, and inner freedom. It is a selfish act that can become a supreme gift of self-love, liberation, and empowerment because we can let go. You don't have to wait for an apology to forgive. If you do, you are still focusing on it; you are not free.

It's all about your inner peace and liberation. It's realizing that grudges from the past rob you of your energy and power and that continuing to hold on is like letting unwanted company live rent-free in your head and heart.

Ultimately, forgiveness is a promise you are making to yourself to not hold the unchangeable past against your present self. It has everything to do with freeing yourself from the burden of being an eternal victim. Forgiveness can feel unfair. But remember, you don't grant forgiveness because somebody deserves it. It's because you deserve it.

While you cannot escape or guard against bad things happening to you, what you can control is how you respond to what happens to you. Often there is the incident, and then there is the story or interpretation of the incident that can keep you in thrall to the wrongdoer or wrongdoing for a long time. Forgiveness is often seen as letting someone off the hook or failing to hold them accountable for their deeds. The primary reason you forgive the person who hurt you is actually very selfish: to set you free from being bound to the wrongdoer and from a lifetime of victimhood.

Forgiveness is a gift that you choose to give to someone who has wronged you. It's an act of grace from you to them. And yet, it is also one of the best gifts you can give to yourself. It allows you to get the closure that you need to let go, move on, and move forward with your life. In the end, it is an act of self-love.

Chapter 19:

Gratitude

Acknowledging the good you already have in your life is the foundation for all abundance. –Eckhart Tolle

***

If you want to experience boundless abundance in your life, commit to cultivating an attitude of gratitude. Practicing gratitude may be at the top of the list of strategies known to boost happiness and life satisfaction, promote good relationships, and benefit physical and mental health. It's about opening up to experiencing the beauty, wonder, and abundance of life. When we feel one with all of life, then we're awake, enlightened, and living in a state of love. Enhancing your well-being, then, may be as simple as taking the time each day to reflect on what you're thankful for.

Every emotion has a frequency to it. And gratitude is the frequency that is harmonious with abundance. The more you are grateful, the more you have. Ultimately, you get what you thank. You tend to attract more of what you are grateful for into your life.

Not all gratitude is equal in its transformative power. There is a gratitude that is conditional—a reactive or knee-jerk gratitude that is based on circumstances. We are grateful only if, when, and because something good happens or when things go our way. It has to be stimulated for it to be felt. It is attached to a condition (something turning out the way you want) or it requires an object, like an expensive gift.

For gratitude to be genuine, to have power, and be sustainable, it needs to be generative, or independent of circumstances or stimuli. Generative gratitude is gratitude for no reason, a no-matter-what chosen gratitude. Example: "I am grateful for my life, for everything I have in my life, and for everything I continue to manifest."

I am grateful for all of life's blessings and all of life's challenges and lessons. I am grateful to be who I am doing what I do and being able to learn, feel, grow, love, and experience happiness and fulfillment. I celebrate the fact that I can generate my own gratitude that is dependent on nothing and no one."

We did not get to where we are in life by ourselves. Circumstances and situations lined up perfectly to get us to where we are right now. It is the understanding that life owes you nothing and all the good you have is a gift.

The same can be said about happiness and love. The power of each also lies in its freedom from circumstances, conditions, stimuli, and reasons. I love you for no reason and not for your looks, your wealth, what you give me, and what you do for me. I am happy in the happiness that I can generate for and by myself. To be happy, I do not need people and things in my life to be a certain way or to turn out a certain way. I am happy knowing that nothing and no one out there can make me happy (or unhappy).

Remember, it is not happiness that brings us gratitude. It's gratitude that brings us happiness. If we are happy no matter what the circumstances in life, in that state, we will definitely move through challenges easier and bounce back quicker than we ever thought possible. And we can generate a sense of gratitude, even when situations and circumstances are not to our liking. It is especially important to be able to generate gratitude in the face of adversity, challenges, and hardships. That would be the best test of how real our gratitude is.

An attitude of nothing missing, for no reason, and no matter what, is what sets us free.

Chapter 20:

Love Expressed in Work

Find your passion and you'll never work a day in your life. –Mark Twain

Far and away the best prize that life has to offer is the chance to work hard at work worth doing. –Theodore Roosevelt

***

How do you express love through work? You can contribute your talents and skills and be of service to this world while doing any job. People often look to their jobs to define their worth. They often look to their earnings, status, and prestige rather than the fulfillment, satisfaction, value, benefit, and contribution derived from the job. But it is possible to find happiness in any job because what you do is often less important than how you do it. Whatever your profession, your worth is inherent to who you are and not what you do for a living.

Anything you either love, care deeply about, or are passionate about, can become a job or a vehicle in which to express and spread your love into the world. It can be the gateway to your spiritual path, self-discovery, and self-actualization. You draw out the "art" contained in "heart."

Anything you love doing, are really good at, and are passionate about or consider important to do can be turned into an art—cooking, healing, building, teaching, speaking, child-rearing, serving, cleaning, consulting, coaching, writing, sewing, painting, inventing, designing, or scrubbing toilets. No job is too menial or ordinary. It is the attitude and the grace with which the person is doing it that counts.

It's not about the job; it's about who you are doing it. Because who you are doing it answers the questions: Whom do I serve? How can I help? How can I better serve? How does this allow me to spread my love, skill, talent, and wisdom to enhance people's lives?

What is the transformation that is possible here—for them and for me? If you have found your purpose or calling in this lifetime, you can consider yourself among the luckiest people alive. If the job brings you joy and fulfillment, is in line with your values, allows you to be authentically you while using your skills and assets to create value and contribute to the quality of people's lives, if what you offer is needed and wanted and you have found a way to monetize it, then you have got it made!

There is no greater blessing than to know that you are here to fulfill your purpose and to share your gift in a way that aligns with your values and can make our world happier, safer, healthier, more peaceful, and more beautiful. I believe no amount of money in the world can quite compare with this feeling of relevance, significance, power, and fulfillment. Rather than constantly running on empty and needing to be filled up with others' love and validation, you yourself become an unending source of love through your giving and sharing.

This is love in action. It becomes a source of courage, strength, and power. You know that what you are doing is important. You are making the world a better place because your product, service, or contribution is the answer to what is needed, wanted, and missing. It is also something you are proud to accept money for because it is a fair exchange for the tremendous value you provide. Or you have understood, identified, and located the pain, and you are providing the gain.

This art of doing business becomes an extension of your spiritual development. This is business from the heart and soul. It is a part of your mission, and it fulfills a deep personal need for purpose, connection, meaning, and for making a difference in the world. There is no shortage of problems to solve or pain to alleviate. We have no shortage of love, caring, generosity, skill, creativity, expertise, and power to solve these problems. This is the transformation from pain to gain. And the more *you* give, the more you gain.

"Follow your bliss" is a phrase popularized by the American mythologist Joseph Campbell, who believed that people should pursue the activities that make them truly happy and fulfilled in life. Campbell argued that when individuals pursue their passions and follow their innate desires, they are more likely to live a fulfilling life and find their true purpose. According to Campbell, the key to following your bliss is to listen to your inner voice and pay attention to your intuition (Campbell, 1949). This may involve taking risks, stepping outside of your comfort zone, and embracing new experiences that challenge you to grow and evolve.

In essence, "following your bliss" is about finding and pursuing what brings you joy and meaning in life, rather than living according to the expectations of others or society at large. It is a call to live authentically, with passion and purpose, and to create a life that reflects your vision, values, unique talents, and aspirations.

Love as expressed in work can take many forms but, at its core, involves passion, pride, dedication, commitment, and care for the work that one does and the people one does it for. When we love our work, we feel energized, fulfilled, and inspired, and we are more likely to bring our best selves to our jobs each day.

One way that love can manifest in work is through a sense of purpose and meaning. When we feel that our work is meaningful and contributes to something larger than ourselves, we are more likely to feel a sense of fulfillment and satisfaction. This can be especially true in careers that involve helping others, such as healthcare, social work, or education.

Love expressed through work involves a deep sense of purpose and passion that drives us to do our best work and make a positive impact on the world around us. It is expressed through creativity and innovation. When we are passionate about our work, we are more likely to come up with new and innovative ideas that can lead to exciting breakthroughs in our fields.

Whatever work you choose, success is when you are clear about the good you put out into the world, and you are happy with what you do and why you do it. To me, there is no greater blessing or wealth.

Love in Business

If you want to go fast, go alone. If you want to go far, go together. —African proverb

Don't aspire to be the best in the team. Aspire to be the best for the team. —Brian Tracy

***

Love in the workplace fosters a deep sense of connection, respect, and support among colleagues. It creates an environment where individuals can thrive both personally and professionally, leading to greater job satisfaction, collaboration, and overall success.

Love in the workplace encourages collaboration and teamwork. It is an environment where colleagues genuinely value and respect each other's contributions. It promotes a culture of inclusivity, where diverse perspectives are embraced, and uniqueness is celebrated. This love cultivates an atmosphere of trust, where individuals can rely on each other, collaborate effectively, and collectively work towards shared goals. It is where when one wins, everyone wins.

There is a culture of recognition and appreciation. People acknowledge and extol each other's achievements, both big and small. It is an environment where compliments, gratitude, and encouragement are freely expressed. This love inspires individuals to excel and provides them with a sense of purpose and significance in their work.

Love in the workplace also involves mentorship and personal growth. It is a setting where experienced colleagues guide and support their junior counterparts, sharing knowledge and helping them develop professionally. This love promotes a learning culture, where it is safe to make mistakes, and where continuous growth and development are encouraged and valued.

Moreover, love in the workplace extends beyond hierarchical boundaries. It is an environment where leaders lead with recognition, compassion and fairness. They genuinely care for the well-being of their team members and create opportunities for their growth and development. This inspires loyalty, motivation, and dedication among employees, leading to increased productivity and personal and organizational success.

Love in the workplace also encompasses work-life balance and well-being. It recognizes the importance of nurturing one's personal life alongside professional responsibilities. It promotes flexible work arrangements, encourages self-care, and supports employees' mental and physical health. This love acknowledges that a healthy and happy workforce is essential for long-term success.

In a workplace filled with love, conflicts are addressed constructively. It is an environment where open and honest communication is encouraged, and disagreements are seen as opportunities for growth and discovery. This love promotes a culture of forgiveness, empathy, and resolution, creating a harmonious and supportive atmosphere.

In conclusion, love in the workplace is a transformative force that transcends mere professionalism. Here empathy, collaboration, recognition, and personal growth thrive. It is a culture that embraces authenticity, inclusivity, and well-being. Love in the workplace not only enhances job satisfaction and productivity but also contributes to the overall happiness and fulfillment of individuals. When love is present in the workplace, it becomes a space where people feel safe and happy and can flourish, realizing their full potential while delivering benefit and value and making a difference in the world.

PART 4
Love Rules

Chapter 21:

The ABCs of a Happy, Healthy, Fulfilling Relationship

Appreciation

Express some form of appreciation and gratitude regularly for your partner and for all the positive aspects of your relationship. Discover newly every day why you love being in this relationship. There are always new things to learn about your partner even after many years. You get more of the good things you focus on. Praise, compliment, and appreciate every chance you get—your partner, your children, your family, and your friends. Make them feel loved, seen, heard, cared for, and cherished. Celebrate their achievements and triumphs. Do it often and sincerely. The more you do it, the more of their qualities you will discover or bring out, the more they will feel significant, and the more grateful you will be to have them in your life. Mignon McLaughlin says: "A successful marriage requires falling in love many times, always with the same person" (Mignon McLaughlin quotes, n.d.).

Boundaries

Clearly communicate and respect each other's personal boundaries.

Some examples of healthy boundaries might include:

- ownership and agency over your financial assets

- the right to privacy and personal space

- the ability to clearly say yes and no as appropriate for staying true to yourself

- the right to your own beliefs, standards, values, preferences, dreams, and goals

- the right to change your mind and to decline anything you don't want to do

- the right to alone time with no distractions or interruptions

Communication

Foster open and honest communication. Dare to share your thoughts, feelings, and pain with each other. Take risks. Daring to be vulnerable can result in greater closeness, safety, and intimacy. Don't play games. Don't expect your partner to read your mind. Say what you need and want. Sometimes an argument gets out of hand. Maybe you forgot to do the "when you do/say, that makes me feel…" thing that we all know we should. If you should find that the difference of views between you has degenerated to this unfortunate and messy point, swallow your pride and be the first to say sorry—simply sorry for allowing things to get overheated, undignified, and out of control, regardless of how righteous you feel about your point of view.

Don't give feedback when triggered. Keep communicating. This is how you stay connected, get to know each other on a deeper level, discover new things about each other, share information, work things out together, break the spell of an impasse, and arrive at true harmony. One of the most loving things you can do is to simply listen attentively to what they have to tell you about what makes them tick, what they think, how they feel, and what is important to them. Be interested and interesting. Avoid mindless chatter. Strive to connect, interest, entertain, inform, share, amuse, illuminate, fascinate, and scintillate.

Let go. Let go of shame, blame, guilt, and pity. Let go of anger and resentment. Let go of needing to be right. Do whatever you need to do or say to move on. Don't waste time staying stuck with feelings of guilt, revenge, or regret. If necessary, apologize, forgive, and make amends; do whatever it takes to let go and set yourself free. You are not responsible for making your partner happy, for fixing them or rescuing them, and vice versa. However, if your partner tells you that something is bothering them and making them unhappy, or they have a special request or need, you take it seriously because you love them and because their unresolved problems and unhappiness will become your problem. See every complaint as a request in disguise. You both need to work together to resolve it so that, in the end, a joint solution is found for the joint problem.

Children

Don't bother having children unless you are prepared to put them first—to arrange your life around them and give them all the love, care, and attention they need and deserve to feel happy, loved, significant, and well-adjusted, to become a valuable contribution to society and to the future, so that they may one day be part of the solution for our planet rather than part of the problem. Children do not come from us; they come through us, and the universe has entrusted some of us with the very important task of providing the children with everything they need to contribute to a world we want to inhabit. Ideally, children should be a free and conscious choice. Your career, hobbies, free time, and everything else take second place. Being a parent can be exhausting and all-consuming, but it is also a very important life mission. Beyond good parenting (where all the child's survival needs are met), our children need to know they are loved, secure, that they matter, and that they come first.

However much responsibility, attention, care, and time your children need and demand from you, they also need to know their parents have a life apart from them, and that they do not sacrifice everything for them. For your children to one day feel free to leave home and find someone else to love, you have to have someone else, too. And that someone else is your partner, from whom you will not have drifted apart, and with whom you will be spending a few more happy decades after your children have left home.

Compromise

Put each other first. When you do this, you are actually putting the relationship first as you worship on the altar of "us." You're saying that the strength and health of the relationship are more important than any one person's needs and wants. You are putting your partner's happiness before your own because, ultimately, you will not be happy if your partner isn't. Many amicable agreements are reached this way after listening and considering each other's viewpoints, preferences, and needs to arrive at a compromise that works for both.

Devotion

Be dedicated to the growth and well-being of your relationship. Always act with integrity, dignity, honor, honesty, compassion, and kindness. Always be the kind of person your partner has every reason to be proud of—the kind of person they never have to cover up for, make excuses for, apologize for, clean up after, or be ashamed of. This is also the kind of person you would want to be in a relationship with.

Notice if you are competing or comparing—either comparing yourself to each other or comparing your relationship to those of others. Remember, you are partners, not opponents or rivals. You are here to support each other, bring out the best in each other, and celebrate each other's happiness, achievements, and good fortune.

Differentiation

Without differentiation, a healthy relationship is simply not possible. This is the ability to maintain one's sense of self and individuality while being emotionally connected. It is about having a sense of autonomy and independence within the relationship without losing one's own identity in the process. It is important for establishing and safeguarding healthy boundaries. It means one is free to pursue one's own interests, goals, and values, and one is more likely to support and encourage the other's personal growth and aspirations. Each is aware of where one ends and the other begins, thereby preventing a collapse into enmeshment, engulfment, and codependency.

Divorce

Once you have done everything and are sure the relationship cannot possibly work out, cut your losses, and get out as soon as you can. Dragging it out will only make things worse and miserable for everyone. Do it for your sanity and dignity. Do it for your children; spare them the acrimony; don't make them pawns in your game. Have the separation be as dignified, amicable, and honorable as possible to minimize the damage as much as you can. Always take the moral high ground; stay decent, kind, and civilized. You will be proud of yourself later that you did not take whatever bait they threw at you. Let go of rancor and feelings of victimhood and revenge. Take responsibility for your part in the break-up so that you do not drag the same issues into a new relationship. It would be preferable if you could stay friends out of love for your children. (I ended my marriage because I felt it was complete. Our paths had diverged, and it was time to move on. The separation was devoid of anger, bitterness, resentment, hostility, or blame. There was just a calm realization that it was the right time to end while we could do so amicably.)

Empathy

Seek to understand your partner's perspective and feelings. Know when to act and when to listen. Sometimes your partner simply needs to be seen, heard, and gotten by you and not for you to come to their rescue, give them advice, fix them, or solve their problem. Listen to what they're telling you, and what they need at the moment will become clear. "What do you think I should do?" means they want advice. When in doubt, ask them, "Do you need my help or advice, or do you just need to get this off your chest?"

Flexibility

Embrace change and be open to compromise. Check that you both have the same shared goals before you make any serious commitment. While you cannot hold your partner to a whole life plan as you can't predict the future, and people and situations can change, you do need a general idea about their views on lifestyle, children, career, where to live, how to care for parents, and all those things that may seem distant now but could make or break your relationship in the long term.

Friends

When it comes to friends, there are no rules. Friendship is not compulsory; it is chosen. You are friends because you have something in common and something to give each other. Maybe they have traits that you admire, or you enjoy their company or find them interesting and fun, and vice versa. Friends can immensely enrich your life, and you can always make room for a new one. Just enjoy them as they come into your life, but know when to let go. Friends are there to make your life better, richer, and happier. There should be more pros than cons, more virtues than faults. In general, you have a feeling of being heard, respected, and supported. You spend time with people you would be proud to become like. You, in turn, need to be the best friend you can possibly be—kind, caring, empathetic, generous, supportive, reliable, and a good listener. Friends do not ask each other to change or behave in certain ways. They are who they are, and you accept them exactly as they are, or you leave. If you find that you or your friend have changed, or you've outgrown the friendship or drifted apart, then it's time to let go and move on. If you find the friendship no longer does anything for you, then you gently withdraw from the friendship.

Growth

Support each other's personal and relational development. Encourage and support your partner (and even more so your children) to fulfill their dreams, to advance and develop, and to be who they want to be, however inconvenient and uncomfortable this might be for you. It might mean they quit their job to enroll in a two-year course or accept a job that takes them away from home most of the time or pursue a different profession or passion. Instead of a point-blank refusal, talk about your concerns, what sacrifices you would be willing to make, and how exactly you can both make this work. (I am fortunate enough to have a partner who supports my goals—I am free to travel alone or to go abroad to volunteer teaching for a month here and there as desired. I regard this as his expression of love and trust.)

Humor

Find joy in shared laughter and use humor to navigate challenges. Whenever possible and appropriate, generously sprinkle in humor, fun, playfulness, silliness, and naughtiness. This can help defuse a tense situation before it gets out of hand. It can make us more tolerant, resilient, and creative in finding new ways of being and seeing other options. We become happier, younger, and more relaxed in the process. (Besides being an ace joke teller and loving to make people laugh, I also love being and acting silly and goofy.)

Imagination

Instead of imagining what kind of partner you want, imagine how you want to feel in a relationship—happy, secure, loved, confident, authentic, empowered, evolved, liberated, and so on. There are many ways to say "I love you" that do not involve money, only imagination and creativity. Beyond the clichéd romantic gestures of flowers, chocolates, fancy dinners, and expensive trips, every little thing they do for you that they don't have to is their way of saying "I love you"—such as washing your car, taking the kids out so you can have a break, giving you a little back massage, making you a cappuccino, and every little unexpected but considerate and caring thing they do for you should be recognized and valued as signs of their love and affection.

Joy

Prioritize activities that bring happiness and fulfillment to both partners. Spend meaningful time together, focusing on the quality of interactions. Go the extra mile to nurture the relationship. Have fun inventing new and creative ways to surprise, amaze, and delight the person you love most in the world. For this, you would mostly need imagination and thoughtfulness. These gestures show them how much you love them, and seeing their pleasure will be your greatest reward.

Kindness

Treat each other with kindness and respect, even in moments of disagreement. Disagree without being disagreeable. Always be kind, courteous, respectful, and thoughtful. Just because you've had a bad day at work doesn't give you the right to take out your anger and frustration on your partner. Before you start dumping, take a few deep breaths and get in touch with what you are feeling, and do your best to calmly share these feelings with your partner.

Perhaps the kindest and most loving thing they can do is simply to listen to you without offering solutions. They might then do something nice for you that they know you would like. They are being caring and empathetic simply because they love you.

Love

Love is a verb—an active commitment continually nurtured and renewed. You have to be willing to do the work. You tend to it like a garden, by giving it the right conditions and nutrients, by clearing the "weeds," to enhance its blossoming and flourishing. By ensuring that you are constantly clearing the "weeds" that choke the life, health, and aliveness out of your relationship, you harvest and reap what you sow.

There is also inner work to be done. The more you know and love yourself, the more you set yourself up for success. Nurture and express your love for each other regularly. By cultivating deep connection, intimacy, closeness, and trust, you provide your relationship with the fertile ground to continuously evolve and deepen. True love is its own reward. It is not a transaction. It is not a give-to-get; it is a give-to-live. It is not conditional or contingent upon anything happening. It is not a quid pro quo or an investment in some future gain. Love is the fullest, truest, most alive, and most beautiful expression of who we are. Spread love, happiness, kindness, compassion, and support as often and as much as you can. See how many smiles you can plant on people's faces. Helping and giving to others is the best way to help and give to yourself. The greater your magnanimity, the more abundant, happy, and fulfilled you are.

Money

Keep your finances separate. After paying joint expenses like rent or mortgage, utilities, everything needed to keep the household running, and children's needs, you both need to agree on what constitutes a fair financial contribution. If one of you doesn't earn anything because you have to stay home to cook, clean, shop, care for the kids, and do all the household chores to enable the other partner to go out and earn money, the earning partner needs to give them fair compensation for their contribution to the partnership, once all essential bills are paid.

After the joint income has been agreed upon, each can keep their share in a separate bank account and is free to do whatever they wish with their money. (In our household, we never fight over finances, because all essential expenses are fairly divided regardless of what each person earns.)

Don't be a Scrooge with your money. Don't be a tightwad, which is another word for mean, which makes you mean instead of generous, giving, and sharing. Don't keep score; don't count and calculate who spent what, when, where, and how much. What's important is how much fun, pleasure, and enjoyment you both derive from it. If you have more money than your partner, then just pay for more—more of the bills, more of the treats, more of everything. You may have to negotiate loaning large sums of money. Other than that, the more you share with the one you love, the more you will get back anyway. After all, you are a team—you both contribute to the wealth, abundance, harmony, and happiness of the partnership.

Nagging

Do not nag, manage, manipulate, control your partner, or tell them what to do, say, or think. You may control your own life, but controlling and making decisions for your partner will undermine their autonomy, confidence, and self-esteem, and will negatively impact your relationship. Do not parent them. This is fine for your children, but not for your partner. Treat your partner as an independent and mature person who is capable of leading their own life and making important decisions and choices on their own. Otherwise, you wouldn't be with them. You are free to express an opinion or tell them about something that bothers you, but do not try to run their lives.

Open-Mindedness

Embrace each other's differences and be open to new ideas. Be more tolerant of your partner's little quirks and foibles, and be aware of your own. We are all imperfect beings having imperfect relationships. We also have different perspectives, different priorities, different personalities, different ideas, different needs, and different ideas about love. We all have habits and faults that may be irritating to the other.

As long as you're not compromising on your most important values, love should get you through the trifles. Perfect doesn't exist. Good enough is good enough. Often, being right and getting your way simply isn't worth the cost of the relationship.

Parents

Stop blaming your parents. Maybe they were not cut out to be parents and never chose to be parents, but they did the best they could with what they had. They are human and might have made mistakes along the way. But they did not do anything bad to you on purpose. Maybe they felt helpless and hopeless as they struggled to cope and to raise you. You become an adult the moment you show understanding and compassion toward them, the moment you get their story, and you let go of blaming them and making them responsible for whatever you didn't get from them. And, as an adult, you no longer need Mommy and Daddy to give you their love, care, attention, approval, affection, and validation. It's now your job to give this to yourself.

Privacy

Respect and safeguard each other's privacy and private space. We all have things we might feel uncomfortable, ashamed, or embarrassed about that we would rather keep to ourselves, and that is our prerogative. And even if we have nothing to hide, we all have a right to privacy and a right to have this right respected. We don't have to give our partner a reason for wanting to be private or needing alone time, despite their threats, pressure, prying, or emotional blackmail. If we are denied this freedom, we will feel controlled and trapped, and this would jeopardize the relationship.

Everyone is entitled to privacy, personal space, secrets, and a certain mystery. None of this concerns us unless it impacts the relationship or unless our partner wants to share it with us. Allow your partner the space to be themselves, to have alone time, to be with other company, and to pursue other interests and hobbies. You would want this for yourself as well. Doing everything everywhere together all the time, no matter how much you may have in common and like each other's company, can be stifling. From time to time, everyone needs to go off and do things on their own, without the other getting jealous, resentful, or feeling rejected, abandoned, or excluded. This is to keep the relationship fresh and to give each other the possibility for new experiences and discoveries to talk to each other about later on. Both parties can retain their own distinct identities, rather than ending up merged into one.

If you refuse them their space, their privacy, and their freedom, it might also result in the end of your relationship. You need to be able to separate to stay together.

Quality Time

You are responsible for the quality of energy you bring into the relationship. Strive to make everything you do come from a space of love, warmth, safety, and comfort, with a smile, hug, and kiss ready. You want you and your partner to always be happy and excited to see each other.

Make your partner a top priority and take every opportunity to remind yourself and them of why you fell in love with them in the first place, and let them know how happy and proud you are to have them in your life. With inventiveness and imagination, regularly and often make time for romance, adventure, fun, passion, and little thoughtful gestures of love (none of these need to involve money) to let them know they are special and cherished. Making your partner's happiness a priority will make you happy.

Relationship

Love your own company. Love your life. First be happy, fulfilled, complete, independent, and secure entirely on your own. You won't be happy with a partner until you can be happy with and by yourself. The only reason you would be in a relationship is because you truly love them and choose to be there, not because you fear being alone or falling apart financially and emotionally without them. You choose to be here because life is simply better with a wonderful person in a loving relationship that does not breed dependence—where both partners are encouraged and supported in coming out stronger, more confident, independent, secure, fulfilled, and happy.

Anyone worth having will love you for yourself—not for your looks, wealth, or status. You want someone deep enough to care about the whole of you. You choose the person who reflects and respects your consciousness and values.

Sex

Make sure that the foundation for your lovemaking is love. When you love someone, sex with them is all about expressing that love in the most personal, intimate, beautiful way possible. It can be as experimental, creative, exciting, and wild as you want, as long as you both want it, but make sure it is caring, respectful, and considerate. Don't go through the motions and use sex as a way to relieve tension or frustration. Instead, be fully present and give them your full attention as you honor and celebrate the gift and privilege it is to express your love for each other in this manner.

Do not mistake lust for love. While great relationships last a lifetime, libido may not. If a relationship is built on sex alone, sooner or later real life kicks in and the relationship's foundation will be tested. Sex may not help you get through the day-to-day struggles and challenges dealing with marriage, children, money, career, in-laws, illness, etc.

Self-Care

Do not let yourself go. Take good care of your health, grooming, and personal hygiene, and make every effort to look and act as attractive as possible. This includes your behavior, language, and actions. You do this out of respect for yourself and your partner, and because this is what you would expect from them as well. They say, "One should never judge a book by its cover," but the reality is, we do! Your appearance affects how others will respond to you and treat you, as well as your own self-image and behavior. You want your partner to consider you the gorgeous, irresistible someone they are proud to be with and be seen with.

Trust

Build and maintain trust through honesty and reliability. Trust that they want the best for you, trust that they can be relied upon, and so on. If you can't trust them, reconsider the relationship. Your partner should not be expected to account for every minute of every day to calm your irrational jealousy. Whatever the reason for your jealousy and suspicion, maybe you've been hurt in the past and now find it impossible to trust, even though your partner has been open and honest about their whereabouts and sympathetic and understanding about your feelings and trust issues, then the jealousy becomes your problem, not theirs. And if you don't get a handle on your jealousy, it may end up destroying your relationship. Do not play games. Do not manipulate people you love; tell them openly and honestly how you feel, what you want, and what's important to you. Relationships based on honesty are the only ones that endure.

Understanding

Strive to comprehend and support each other's needs, values, dreams, and aspirations. Everyone wants to feel seen, heard, and gotten. Be curious. Even after many years of being together, don't assume you know everything about your partner—their tastes, their preferences, their reactions, their fears, and their thoughts and feelings. They don't know everything about you, either. You are two different people, who continue to change and evolve, and you should not assume or expect the other to think or react in a certain way. (I once treated my partner to a variety show only to find that he hated it.) There is a reason for their seemingly irrational and unexpected behavior. You need to find out what triggered this reaction and put yourself in their shoes so your feelings of resentment and frustration can be replaced by sympathy and understanding.

Value

Know your value, which doesn't appreciate or depreciate based on someone's ability to see and acknowledge it. Stop running after acknowledgment, approval, and validation. Make true the attributes you want to be true about you. Always go where you are respected, wanted, and appreciated. Your value appreciates from being appreciated.

Workload

Always share the workload. (In our household, we've arranged it so that this is never an issue because we have a clear division of labor. I do the cooking; he does the washing up. I gather up all the trash; he takes it down. I do the laundry and clean the bathrooms; he does the vacuuming. We both do food shopping. We both keep the place clean and tidy so that we spend as little time as possible on housework.

Everything feels fair and balanced.) Many men think that because they work at a tough job and earn all the money while their wives just stay home with the kids, they shouldn't be expected to contribute to housework as well. Maybe these guys should take a few days off to try this out to see how physically and emotionally draining taking care of the household and pre-school kids can be. Furthermore, the fact that the wife is there to make the house a home, to raise the family, and to tackle all the household chores is what frees him to go out to earn the money.

(E)Xpectations

Discuss together your expectations of the relationship and of each other beforehand. Make those expectations conscious but know it is not your partner's job to fulfill them. Do not go into a relationship to change someone. Either accept them exactly as they are or leave. There may be minor irritations you can live with, like general untidiness, and there are the deal-breakers like alcoholism, gambling, or physical abuse. They might change on their own and become better people over time, but don't count on it. The changes we make for ourselves are the only permanent ones.

Choose to be there or get out. Choice is the key word here—this is your true freedom and power. Stop blaming, complaining, and making anything or anyone else responsible for how you got to where you are. If you stay, then choose to be happy, to be in this relationship, to love this person, your life, your work, and your children. You are responsible for generating your own happiness, gratitude, and self-love. Stop outsourcing it to someone or something to provide it. Accepting responsibility for your life is immensely empowering and liberating as it allows you to choose the outcome you want and work towards it.

Yourself

Love yourself first. You are the most important relationship of your life. You have to love, respect, value, and appreciate yourself before you can love, respect, value, and appreciate another, and before you can receive love from others. It is your job now as an adult to give yourself all the love and whatever else you think you were missing from childhood. As an adult, no one can or should do this for you.

It is very hard to have a healthy relationship with someone who considers themselves unlovable. Don't look for external proof that you are lovable. Just declare it to be so. No one can prove otherwise.

Dare to be authentically you. You are not meant to blend in; you are meant to stand out. You cannot reinvent yourself every time you meet someone you like by trying to become someone you think they are looking for. Otherwise, you will lock yourself into a game of pretense by hiding behind a sham personality that will be hard to keep up long term. You will also be putting out a message that something is wrong or unacceptable about you. You deserve someone who loves you for who you are, not for who you are pretending or trying to be, and not for who they need you to be. Someone out there wants exactly the kind of person you already are, who regards your imperfections as natural, lovable, and charming.

Zeal

Approach the relationship with enthusiasm, passion, joie de vivre, ardor, magic, verve, and a positive attitude. Keep the spark alive by continuously expressing desire and affection. Become a person who's fun, easy, exciting, interesting, and a joy to live with.

Author Bio

Rachel Lin is an international success coach dedicated to guiding her clients toward uncovering their potential and pursuing their heart's desires. She has been transforming lives for over 30 years, empowering individuals to live out their truth, power, and greatness.

rachel-lin-books.com

****

Thank you so much for reading my book. If you enjoyed it, please consider leaving a review on Amazon.

References

Albert Einstein quotes. (n.d.). GoodReads. https://www.goodreads.com/author/quotes/9810.Albert_Einstein

Alexander Pope quotes. (n.d.). GoodReads. https://www.goodreads.com/author/quotes/25157.Alexander_Pope

Angshuman & Bhaswati. (2024, July 17). *150 effective teamwork quotes to spur unity & collaboration.* Vantage Circle. https://www.vantagecircle.com/en/blog/teamwork-quotes/

Bernard M. Baruch quotes. (n.d.). GoodReads. https://www.goodreads.com/author/quotes/5768330.Bernard_M_Baruch#

Campbell, J. (1949, June 10). *The hero with a thousand faces.* Princeton University Press.

Domestic violence statistics. (n.d.). National Domestic Violence Hotline. https://www.thehotline.org/stakeholders/domestic-violence-statistics/

Dominguez, J. & Robin, V. (1992, September 1). *Your money or your life.* Penguin Books.

Eckhart Tolle quotes. (n.d.). GoodReads. https://www.goodreads.com/author/quotes/4493.Eckhart_Tolle

Fairbairn, W. R. D. (1952, December 1). *Psychoanalytic studies of the personality.* Routledge.

Heinlein, R. A. (1991, October 1). *Stranger in a strange land.* Ace.

Huecker, M. R., King, K. C., Jordan, G. A., & Smock, W. (2023, April 9). *Domestic violence.* National Library of Medicine. https://www.ncbi.nlm.nih.gov/books/NBK499891/#

Joan Crawford quotes. (n.d.). GoodReads. https://www.goodreads.com/author/quotes/76857.Joan_Crawford

John Holmes quotes. (n.d.). GoodReads. https://www.goodreads.com/author/quotes/152507.John_Holmes#

Katherine Hepburn quotes. (n.d.). GoodReads. https://www.goodreads.com/author/quotes/84099.Katharine_Hepburn#

Maraboli, S. (2013, May 7). *Unapologetically you: Reflections on life and the human experience.* Better Today.

Mark Twain quotes. (n.d.). BrainyQuote. https://www.brainyquote.com/authors/mark-twain-quotes

Mark Twain quotes. (n.d.). GoodReads. https://www.goodreads.com/author/quotes/1244.Mark_Twain

Mignon McLaughlin quotes. (n.d.). BrainyQuote. https://www.brainyquote.com/authors/mignon-mclaughlin-quotes

Oscar Wilde quotes. (n.d.). GoodReads. https://www.goodreads.com/author/quotes/3565.Oscar_Wilde

Oscars. (2022, May 3). Will Smith wins best actor for 'King Richard' | 94th Oscars [Video]. YouTube. https://www.youtube.com/watch?v=7CX7jmZvytA

Oxford University Press. (n.d.). *Toxic*. Oxford Languages. https://languages.oup.com/google-dictionary-en/

Parton, D. (1974). *When someone wants to leave* [Song]. On Jolene. RCA Records.

Pema Chödrön quotes (n.d.). GoodReads. https://www.goodreads.com/author/quotes/8052.Pema_Ch_dr_n

Robert A. Heinlein quotes. (n.d.). GoodReads. https://www.goodreads.com/author/quotes/205.Robert_A_Heinlein

Rumi quotes. (n.d.). GoodReads. https://www.goodreads.com/quotes/582645-love-is-the-whole-thing-we-are-only-pieces

RuPaul. (2024). *RuPaul teaches self-expression and authenticity [Online course]*. MasterClass. https://www.masterclass.com/classes/rupaul-teaches-self-expression-and-authenticity

Saxe, J. G. (1873). *The blind men and the elephant*. CommonLit. https://www.commonlit.org/en/texts/the-blind-men-and-the-elephant

St. Francis de Assisi quotes (n.d.). GoodReads. https://www.goodreads.com/author/quotes/149151.Francis_of_Assisi#

Theodore Roosevelt quotes. (n.d.). GoodReads. https://www.goodreads.com/author/quotes/44567.Theodore_Roosevelt

Whitby, A. (2020, December 25). *Who first said: if you want to go fast, go alone; if you want to go far, go together?* Andrew Whitby. https://andrewwhitby.com/2020/12/25/if-you-want-to-go-fast/

Printed in Great Britain
by Amazon